Star
Running Backs
Of The NFL

The triumphs and setbacks of some of the greatest runners in modern professional football. Included are profiles of Floyd Little, Leroy Kelly, Dick Bass, O. J. Simpson, Gale Sayers, Alvin Haymond, Ron Johnson, Calvin Hill, Duane Thomas, Larry Brown and others.

STAR
RUNNING BACKS
OF THE NFL

by Bill Libby

Illustrated with photographs

RANDOM HOUSE
NEW YORK

For RUTH and LOU

PHOTOGRAPH CREDITS: Malcolm Emmons: front and back end-papers, 1, 27, 52, 106, 115, 128; Emmons and Brockway, ii, 9; Ken Regan—Camera 5: 64, 85; Fred Roe—Photography Unlimited: 92; United Press International: i, 5, 12, 22–23, 30, 41, 48, 56, 68, 73, 75, 79, 87, 109, 112, 119, 125, 132–133, 137, 139; Wide World: 16, 36, 44, 59, 72, 82, 96, 100, 123.
COVER: Ken Regan—Camera 5.

Published under license from National Football League Properties, Inc.

Trade Edition: ISBN: 0–394–82285–4
Library Edition: ISBN: 0–394–92285–9

Library of Congress Catalog Card Number: 77–158376

Manufactured in the United States of America

CONTENTS

ACKNOWLEDGMENTS

FOR THEIR HELP in providing the material for this book, the author wishes to thank the subjects themselves most sincerely, as well as Don Weiss, Jim Heffernan, Harold Rosenthal and Regina Henry of the National Football League; Dick Maxwell of the Denver Broncos; Don Smith of the New York Giants; Nate Wallack of the Cleveland Browns; Jack Nicholson of the Boston Patriots; Jerry Wynn of the San Diego Chargers; Jack Horrigan of the Buffalo Bills; Charles Callahan of the Miami Dolphins; Joe Pollack of the St. Louis Cardinals; Jerry Wilcox and Jack Geyer of the Los Angeles Rams; Elliott Trumbull of the Dallas Cowboys; Lyall Smith of the Detroit Lions; Joe Blair of the Washington Redskins; the many fine writers who have written in the past about the stars profiled in the following pages; and the photographers who took the pictures which illustrate this book.

INTRODUCTION

THIS IS the age of the passer in pro football. The star quarterbacks who throw the ball attract the most attention today, whereas once it was the great running backs from Red Grange through Jimmy Brown. Yet, runners remain critical to any team's success, and it is the running back who still provides the greatest thrills in the game.

Few long passes are as exciting as a long run. It is impossible to watch the passer and all his potential receivers at the same time. However, you can follow the runner all the way. The most excitement in any highlight film is provided by the spectacular runner.

In *Star Running Backs of the NFL*, we profile many of the standout ball-carriers of recent years. Most of them are still active. Some of them are champion runners of the past or present. Some of them are probably title-winning runners of the future. Each has a unique style and a unique story of his own. All had to overcome obstacles to gain success. Not all have been fortunate enough to play on winning teams. But all have been outstanding.

Football itself has been changing. Expansion has added many new cities to the pro sport. The old National Football League merged with the new American Football League after the latter's 10-year existence. And in 1970 the NFL was divided up into National and American Conferences with three divisions of teams in each. Runners once sought NFL or AFL titles. Now they go for NFC or AFC titles. But the accomplishments are no less.

Every year pro football players get bigger and faster, it seems. The running back takes terrible punishment. Many prominent ones are injured every season. Some outstanding careers have been curtailed. Yet, other star ball-carriers have come back from injury to play gallantly. Some of those we profile in this book have been hurt in the past. Some will be hurt in the future. But all have earned attention.

What could top running 60 or 80 yards through an entire opposing team to a spectacular touchdown with a great stadium full of fans on their feet and cheering you? The great players in this book have done this.

STAR
RUNNING BACKS
OF THE NFL

FLOYD LITTLE

· 1 ·

IT WAS MID-SEASON 1969, and Floyd Little had finally come of age as a pro football runner. After two ordinary seasons with the Denver Broncos, the former Syracuse University All-American now led the American Football League in rushing. Despite missing one full game with an injury, he had rushed for more than 500 yards, averaging more than five yards a carry. The tough, tricky little stylist had gained a place at the top.

It was the night before a game with San Diego. Joyce Little, his wife, beat Floyd seven games to five on the pool table in the basement of their Denver home. They hovered over the table like hustlers, wisecracking, but serious. Floyd laughed, "She gets me in the mood for winning at football by beating me at pool."

He watched TV for a while, fell asleep about 11, then slept until 11 the next morning. He skipped breakfast, as he always did on the day of a game, because food did not feel good in his stomach when he was nervous. He grew more nervous as his wife drove him to Mile High Stadium and the game drew near.

It had snowed on Saturday and more snow swirled down now as he entered the dressing room. He had his legs rubbed down and his ankles taped while the other players drifted in, clowning to cut the tension. They pulled on their bulky gear and their red and white uniforms and then sat quietly as their coach, Lou Saban, talked to them about how to beat the Chargers.

Finally, it was time. Floyd pulled on his blue helmet and ran out onto the field with the rest of the Broncos. It had stopped snowing, but the sidelines were white, and the field, which had been covered with a tarpaulin and had lost its grass, was brown. It was a dark day, so the overhead arc lights were turned on.

The Broncos played in a minor league baseball stadium which had been improved and expanded with double-decker stands along one sideline. Football did not draw big crowds here in the early 1960s, when Denver was one of the worst teams in the new AFL. But now the team had improved and the AFL was planning to merge with the older NFL. Mile High Stadium usually held full houses of more than 45,000 persons. Today was no different.

At 5-foot-10 and 195 pounds, Little *seemed* little among the giants who were warming up for combat,

In a game against Oakland, Denver's Floyd Little carries the ball over a pile-up at the line.

but he grew in stature as the game began. At first he was used sparingly. The Denver quarterback would fake to Floyd, whom the Chargers were watching, then give to another back. When Little did get the ball, he moved it, darting quickly through openings in the line, shifting speeds smoothly, faking out defenders with jitterbug steps, breaking tackles with surprising strength, and pushing forward for extra yardage.

"Fluid" was the word that kept coming to mind when you watched him. He ran hard, but with fluid motion, breaking a hard tackle to get 21 yards on one run. He reached out to catch a long pass on his fingertips and pivoted away from two defenders to get 17 yards on another play.

Twice, pass interceptions stalled Denver drives. Little made the tackle after one of those interceptions. "I love those tackles, I love contact," he said later. "Why should I be taking the raps? I'd rather be hitting them than having them hit me."

There was no scoring until the Broncos took command in the second half. Passes produced one touchdown. Another score was set up when Little shook loose on a screen pass for 21 yards. Then Floyd himself rammed the ball home from two yards out. He and his mates on the offensive team trooped happily to the bench.

Late in the third quarter Little took another screen pass for a 15-yard gain, but he was tackled viciously by Ken Graham. Floyd writhed in pain on the frozen ground and was finally carried to the bench. As a doctor worked on his right leg, someone helped him off with his helmet, revealing his face, numb from cold and caked with mud.

He did not get back into the game, which ended as a two-touchdown triumph for Denver. The weary Broncos trotted jubilantly into their dressing room under the outfield bleachers as the chilled fans stood and cheered them. Little limped in last.

He stripped and hobbled into the trainer's room, where he sat on a table with his legs spread and his back pressed against the wall. Despite his injury, he was smiling. All around him the players whooped and hollered in the steamy warmth.

Little's shins were scabbed from old sores and scraped bloody with new ones. "Badges of battle," he said, grinning. He pressed an ice pack against a large bruise on his right thigh, but it was his knee that worried him. It had been twisted severely, and he was told he would have to have it examined the following day.

"The tackler was so close to me I didn't think he could hit me heavy," Floyd explained. "If I had lowered my head and just rammed into him, I'd never have been hurt. But I knew another touchdown would put us out of reach, and I could see that if I could get by this one tackler, I'd go, so I began to put down some stuff. He wasn't fooled and hit me hard while I had both feet off the ground. I landed awkwardly and knew I was hurt."

The players drifted in to console him, sorry he was hurt but still happy with their victory. The Broncos had reached the .500 level with a 4–4 record, a height they had attained only once before in their

10-year history. Little probed his sore knee gently with his scuffed-up fingers and shrugged his shoulders. "You can't tip-toe through games. If you're cautious, you're through. You go all out and hope for the best."

Earlier in his career he had been handicapped by a cracked collarbone, a wrenched back, a sprained ankle and a severely lacerated finger. He also had been slowed down by a bad siege of flu and twice was weakened by spells of iron deficiency.

He got up from the table and limped into the shower-room. Although he was not a big man, he was thickly muscled. He also had severely bowed legs. "They help me," he grinned. "They're so bowed, tacklers can't get their arms all the way around them. If they were straight, I'd be three inches taller and a great pass receiver."

He returned, drying himself off. Most of the other players had departed by then. Painfully, Floyd dressed, pulling on slacks, a white turtleneck sweater and a heavy coat. He went out into the darkness, for it was night now, and even colder than it had been during the game. A group of youngsters stood outside by the dressing room door, waiting for him to sign autographs. He stopped and gave them out patiently.

Someone called, "Hey, Floyd, your wife says to hurry before she freezes to death." Floyd grinned and limped to the sidelines where she waited, dancing from foot to foot and clapping her hands in an effort to keep warm. "Oh, baby, beautiful," she said, hugging and kissing him. Then her victory smile

Floyd Little.

faded, her face grew concerned and she asked him, "Are you hurt bad?" He said he thought it was all right. She was relieved.

Unfortunately, the injury turned out to be more serious than expected. It did not require an operation, like so many knee injuries in pro football, but Floyd's leg was in a cast for a long time. In the meantime Little got around on crutches and missed four games. "Those were the worst four weeks of my life," he said later. "I lost eight or nine pounds worrying."

He had been so far ahead in the rushing statistics that it was the fourth week before another runner on the circuit moved ahead of him in yards gained. Floyd returned for the final two games, but he was far below form. He finished fifth in rushing, winding up with 729 yards on 146 attempts for a five-yard average.

After Little was hurt, Denver failed to win in its next five games and won again only in the last game of the season. Little said, "It's a deep disappointment, but you have to learn to handle disappointment in sports. You have to keep trying your best and hope things will get better."

Floyd Douglas Little was born on the Fourth of July, 1942, in Waterbury, Connecticut. His father died of cancer when Floyd was six, leaving Floyd's mother to raise six children on $3,200 a year in welfare payments. They lived in a poor, black section of town and had few luxuries.

Floyd was a homely, nervous child, who for a long time would venture out into the world only when he could hang onto an older sister's skirt. The other children nicknamed him "Cheetah" (after Tarzan's chimp) and mocked him. When he mispronounced a word in the third grade and others laughed at him, he refused to read aloud in school for many years afterwards.

His mother moved her family to New Haven when Floyd was 13. There they settled in another ghetto.

In one house in which they lived, there were 26 children on three floors. There was little hope for the future of any of them. Floyd, however, found hope in sports.

He was a fast, agile youngster, who played all games brilliantly. Unfortunately, he was too busy making a badly-needed $5 a day as a shoeshine boy to practice with his teams. He got to Hillhouse High School late, learned little there, and became too old to play high school football before he finished school. But by then he was already established as a great football prospect.

Many colleges offered Little football scholarships. He could not imagine himself in college, so he sought work. He applied for a job as a janitor but was rejected when he was unable to fill out the application properly. The company considered him illiterate.

Bordentown Military Academy, a college preparatory school, was seeking a black athlete to integrate the school. They offered Floyd a scholarship and he accepted. He played brilliant football for them and they worked hard on giving him an education. "There was nothing wrong with my mind, but no one had reached out to help me before," he explained. "With help, I began to do well in my studies. Finally, I felt I could make it in college."

Many colleges sought him, including Syracuse, which sent its All-America runner, Ernie Davis, to recruit him. Davis, a simple, honest person, who was seriously sick with leukemia, impressed Little deeply. Floyd was undecided which school to accept

Playing for Syracuse University in November 1966, Little scores a touchdown against Florida State and breaks the all-time Syracuse record for rushing yardage.

until the day Davis died. Little then telephoned Syracuse coach Ben Schwartzwalder to tell him he had a new running back.

At Syracuse Little was given the number 44 of his immortal predecessors, Jim Brown and Davis. Floyd surpassed their accomplishments there, gaining 2,704 yards rushing and totalling nearly 5,000 yards running, returning kicks, passing and catching passes. He scored as many as five touchdowns and gained as many as 216 yards in one game.

A spectacular breakaway runner, Floyd became one of the few players to attain All-America honors three straight seasons. And he helped his team to great success. He blossomed as an inspirational leader who often voluntarily tongue-lashed lagging teammates on behalf of his coach.

A campus celebrity, Floyd also blossomed in the classroom, studying history and religion and reading and writing poetry, which he came to love. He also came to love Joyce Green, a lovely daughter of a New York schoolteacher. Joyce stepped up her program in order to graduate with Floyd and finished in just three years, with honors. After graduation they were married.

Little called college the redeeming experience of his life and he said he was depressed by those who seem to spend more time protesting the system than profiting by it. He said, "It used to bug me to sweat for hours over books for C's, while others fooled around and got A's; but I had a lot of catching up to do and I may have gotten more from my studies than those to whom everything came easy. While others could take jobs for extra money, I had to attend summer school. I was an old senior, 25. But I remember sitting in class and looking around and marvelling that I had become a member of the elite. And while a lot of athletes never graduate, I did, and in four years."

The year he graduated was the first year of the merger between the NFL and AFL. In previous years pro prospects could get offers from both leagues and take the higher offer. Floyd had no choice but to go to the one team which drafted him for whatever it offered him. Denver drafted Floyd and signed him to a four-year contract worth about $130,000.

Although others had received more, Little admitted it would have been unreasonable for him to complain about his contract since he had never dreamed of making that much earlier. He was disappointed at first to have to play for a poor team in a town that he imagined to be a small place in the wilds, but he and Joyce swiftly learned to love Denver and Floyd soon was dedicated to helping make the team a winner.

Floyd's first year with the Broncos was also the first in Denver for coach Lou Saban, a tough, determined man who had brought Buffalo a championship a few years earlier. Saban dropped most of the Bronco veterans and began the 1967 season with 11 rookies and 25 others who had three years or less experience.

A 26-year-old rookie, Little had his troubles. Running behind inexperienced blockers, he averaged less than three yards a carry, had no run longer than 14 yards and totalled only 381 yards. He made many mistakes and fumbled frequently. His true ability emerged only in solo performances. He returned one kickoff 59 yards and one punt 72 yards, led the league in kickoff returns with 942 yards, and was among the leaders in punt returns with 272 yards. The team won only three games, however, and Little was considered a disappointment.

In his second pro season, 1968, Floyd was injured early and remained disappointing until November. He began to break through in the last half of the schedule. One Sunday he gained 126 yards against Miami. The next Sunday he rushed for 147 yards against Boston. On one play he took a pitchout, reversed his field and raced 55 yards to score. A week later he returned a kickoff 89 yards against Oakland. The next week he carried back a punt 67 yards against Houston.

Perhaps he proved himself as a pro against Buffalo. He caught a pass for a 66-yard score to help the Broncos to a 31–29 lead with less than a minute to play. Then he fumbled deep in his own territory. The Bills recovered and kicked a field goal to go ahead 32–31 with only 26 seconds to play.

Frustrated and furious, Little pleaded for the opportunity to atone. "All I knew was 40 guys had worked their tails off for almost 60 minutes to win and then one guy had blown it all in one second," he recalled.

After the kickoff the Broncos had the ball deep in their own territory. Floyd's number was called on a pass play. He faked free, caught the ball, and gained

66 yards before being downed. Bobby Howfield rushed on to kick a field goal giving Denver a dramatic 34–32 triumph. Floyd wept with joy.

He completed the season with 584 yards rushing, averaging 3.7 yards per carry, 331 yards on pass receptions and 910 yards returning punts and kickoffs. No one in football surpassed his more than 1,800 yards in total running offense. But the team had improved only slightly, winning five games.

In 1969 Little gained 105 yards in the opening victory over Boston and 104 yards in the following conquest of New York. In the latter game the Broncos had fallen behind 13–0 when Little went back to receive a punt. He said to Bill Thompson, the other deep receiver, "We need a big play." Then he took the punt at the Denver 47 and returned it to the one-yard-line. On the next play he smashed over for the touchdown.

He was injured late in the New York game and missed the next game, but returned against Kansas City to gain 63 yards running, 56 returning kicks and 70 catching passes—on a rain-soaked, muddy field. Then he rushed for 92 against Oakland. At Cincinnati he exploded for 166 yards in 29 carries, including a flashy 48-yard scoring effort in which he reversed his field twice and faked out two tacklers to score the key points in a 30–23 triumph.

In the Houston Astrodome Floyd rushed for 65 yards and carried a screen pass 39 yards to set up a late rally. He also threw a perfect pass that Mike Haffner dropped as he ran into the end zone. That touchdown would have won the game—Denver lost

New York Jet defenders fail to stop Little on a plunge from the one-yard-line. Denver won the game 21–19.

by three points. Then came the San Diego game in which Little was injured. He concluded the 1969 campaign with 729 yards rushing and 218 yards receiving passes.

In 1969 the Bronco bosses had begun to protect him from injury by keeping him off the kick-return teams. In 1970 they continued this strategy by throwing fewer passes to him and using him less often on tight line-plunges. He began the season healthy again, and the Broncos got off to a fast start. They won their first three games and four of their first five. Then things started to fall apart. They won only one game and tied only one the rest of the way.

However, Little remained effective most of the season. His best game was against the powerful San Francisco 49ers when he gained 180 yards, including an exciting 80-yard scoring run.

Little was approaching his first 1,000-yard season when he broke a bone in his back in the 12th game. Though not too serious, the injury was painful, and it handicapped him in the last two contests. He fell short of the 1,000-yard mark, but he still won the American Football Conference rushing crown, his first, finishing the season with 901 yards in 209 attempts for an average of more than four yards per carry.

He received more votes than any player on the conference All-Star Team and was named All-Pro for the entire NFL. After four injury-plagued professional seasons he had entered his prime and earned recognition as perhaps the top running back in the game. "Individual recognition is just great," he admitted, "but it doesn't mean as much when your team hasn't done well. I'll just have to keep trying to do more and hope it helps my team do better."

Off the field Floyd had become a poised, articulate person. One summer he worked on Colorado Governor John Love's staff as a consultant on minority group problems. He went into depressed areas, found out what the people needed most and tried to set up programs to fill those needs. He admitted he grew depressed because solutions were hard to find and hard to put into practice.

He said he would like to go into youth counselling in the future. "I am not a militant and I do not believe in violence. I do not believe a person should waste his time in college creating turmoil," he said. "I am black and proud of it. I'd like to work with black boys, with minority groups, with all boys who have a hard time getting started. If I had been counselled, I wouldn't have left high school too dumb to fill out an application for a job as a janitor. I'm one who knows now how much good college can do for a person. I'd also like to coach because I love football.

"Basically, I'm an old-fashioned sort. I believe in old-fashioned virtues. I believe in doing right. I believe in making the most of your God-given abilities. I'm a natural-born runner. It's something I do well and I've worked to become better at it. I believe in becoming the best you can at the things you do best, whether it's playing a game, singing, selling something or working on cars. I feel fortunate that what I do well is glamorous and exciting and pays well. I've had to endure a lot of injuries, but that's part of it."

In the age of the passer there is still room for the runner, the most exciting performer on the football field. Floyd Little had become one of the great ones.

LEROY KELLY

·2·

1968 WAS the second successive season Leroy Kelly had led the National Football League in rushing. It was also the year the brilliant Cleveland ball-carrier finally moved out from under the shadow of the retired Jimmy Brown.

Late in the season the Cleveland Browns, in contention for the Century Division crown, were battling Minnesota. Minnesota led 10–0 until the Browns rallied with a drive climaxed by a short plunge by Kelly to cut the deficit to 10–7. With less than four minutes remaining, the Browns recovered a fumble on Minnesota's 47-yard-line and Kelly went to work.

Taking a handoff from the quarterback, Leroy swung wide to his left, got in behind his blockers, ripped right through a tackler, cut down the sidelines and sped to the 11-yard-line before being shoved out of bounds.

The quarterback called Kelly's number again. On a play designed to complement the previous sweep,

Kelly came from his right, took the handoff, and started to run left. The middle linebacker followed in the same direction. Then Leroy planted his left foot and made a sharp cut down the middle. He burst through a hole in the line and knifed into the area vacated by the linebacker, who was trying desperately to get back into position. Kelly drove all the way to the three.

On the next play he swept to the opposite side, moving the ball to within one foot of the goal line. Then, on his fourth consecutive carry, he went back to the left and dove over the massed line for the winning touchdown.

This was Leroy Kelly at his best. One of the quickest starters off his marks in football history and able to make some of the sharpest cuts, Kelly ran outside or inside with equal ability. Sometimes he shook loose on long runs, but more often he piled up yardage with five- to fifteen-yard bursts.

Jim Brown probably was the greatest running back in football history. In nine seasons between 1957 and 1965 he had carried the ball more often (2,359 times) and gained more yards (12,312) than any back ever. He also held the season records with 305 carries and 1,863 yards. In 58 separate games Brown gained 100 yards or more. He led the NFL in rushing eight times, five times in a row.

Kelly had succeeded Brown in the Cleveland backfield and found Brown's shoes hard to fill. He did not match Brown's records, but he was one of the most successful ballcarriers of his era. He gained 1,000 yards or more in three straight seasons, passed

Leroy Kelly (44) of the Cleveland Browns follows teammate John Demarie (65) around left end in a game against the Minnesota Vikings.

the 5,000-yard milestone in total yards rushing during 1970, and led the league in rushing two years in a row.

"I was supposed to be another Jimmy Brown. But who could be?" asked Kelly. "All I ever wanted to be was Leroy Kelly, the best ballplayer and the best person I could be. When I finally began to get recognition on my own, I was very grateful and relieved. It was a kind of hard pull in life for me to become my own man."

Leroy was born May 20th, 1942, in the black "Nicetown" section of North Philadelphia. His father was a mechanic in a lime factory and a former semi-pro baseball player who worked hard to provide a fair life for his brood.

Kelly had athletically-inclined older brothers who set the pace for him. The first two Kelly sons were named Samson and Ulysses. The next two were given the less glamorous names of Leroy and Harold. They grew up next to Fern Hill Park. "We'd get out to the park with the first light of morning," Leroy recalled. "All day we'd play baseball, basketball, football, whatever. A lot of ghettos don't have parks. We were lucky."

He and one of his brothers formed a teen-age gang they called "The Birds," and they often got into brawls with rival gangs. But as they grew up, they found they could excel in athletics, so they concentrated on sports rather than fights. All the brothers played baseball, basketball and football at Simon Gratz High School. Leroy earned nine letters there.

The older Kelly brothers went to work early and did not try out as pro athletes. Leroy himself passed up pro baseball to work summers. Harold, nicknamed "Pat," the youngest of the brothers, did go into baseball and made the major leagues as an outfielder.

Leroy found his place in football. He was a quarterback who ran more than he passed. He also kicked off, punted, ran back kickoffs and punts, played middle linebacker on defense and made half his team's tackles.

"He did everything for us," recalled his high school coach, Louis DeVicaris. "We didn't have anyone who could catch a pass. I told him to count to three and if no one was open, to take off and run. Once he ran on fourth down from our own two-yard-line and went 98 yards for a touchdown.

"He was the most vicious tackler you can imagine. He'd lift a guy, carry him three yards back and dump him on the ground. Sure I worried about him, but I felt like he'd never get hurt. We'd just tape him up and send him out there. He was the greatest football player I ever saw."

Despite his high school performance, few major colleges offered Leroy football scholarships on his graduation. His high school specialty had been auto mechanics, and few coaches felt he could do well enough in his studies to stay in college. His coach finally landed him a partial scholarship at Morgan State, the black college in Baltimore. Leroy worked full-time to earn the additional money he needed. He graduated with a Bachelor of Science degree.

At Morgan State Kelly's coach, Earl Banks, converted him from a quarterback to a halfback. "He could throw long, but not short. He could loop the long ones, but he couldn't throw the short ones hard enough to break a pane of glass," said Banks. "But he could run. And he could catch the ball. And he could kick it. He also could play defensive back brilliantly."

Kelly was a fine back, if not a great one, at Morgan. He still was maturing physically and weighed little more than 180 pounds. As a senior he averaged more than five yards a carry and was the team's third best rusher and pass-catcher. He was voted the team's most valuable player in the post-season Orange Blossom Bowl game, an annual duel between black powers. Morgan State met Florida A&M and lost 30–7.

The pro teams were not enormously impressed by Kelly. Buddy Young, a great pro running back and a scout, tried to interest the Baltimore Colts in taking a chance on Leroy, but they weren't interested. Young called Cleveland, but the Browns were only slightly more interested. There were several other running backs they wanted more. But before their first turn came around, their first choices had been taken by other teams. At first the disappointed Browns chose players at other positions. Finally, in the eighth round, after more than a hundred players had been chosen, Cleveland called Kelly's name. Personnel Director Paul Bixler admitted he wasn't sure if Leroy would be tried out as a runner, a receiver or a defensive back.

Cleveland coach Blanton Collier observed Kelly and other rookies at a summer tryout camp in 1964 and told him, "You look like you might make it as a runner, but I wish you were heavier." Leroy said, "Don't worry, I'll build up." Eating instead of exercising, Kelly went from 188 to 202 pounds by the time he reported. However, he was not in shape and soon pulled a leg muscle, which reduced his chances of making the team enormously. Anyway, the Browns already had great regular running backs with Jim Brown at fullback and Ernie Green at halfback. Even with this competition and with his injury, Leroy showed enough potential to be kept as a reserve runner.

For two seasons Kelly played primarily on the "special teams" that return kickoffs and punts. He carried the ball from scrimmage only six times his first season and only 37 times his second season. He didn't catch a single pass his first season, and only nine his second season. Like many who later became

Kelly relaxes on the sidelines.

stars, Kelly spent several unremarkable years before he got a chance to prove himself. No doubt, some potential greats never get the chance.

Kelly attracted attention, though, by returning kickoffs and punts, some for spectacular long gains. Although he was seldom used from scrimmage, he gained more than 1,500 yards his first two seasons. He was also noticed for his heavy tackling covering punts and kickoffs. Coach Blanton Collier said of Kelly, "He was called upon to do a lot of things. He demonstrated that he was a fine all-around athlete. He proved himself a fine team man. When Brown retired, he'd earned the chance to replace him."

Kelly recalled that he was awed by Brown when he first joined the team. He remembered that when he first met Brown, all he got from the great veteran was an icy stare. He said it was a week before Brown spoke to him. His first words were, "Hey rookie, run over there and get us a couple of footballs." Yet Leroy noted, "I learned just by watching him. I really wasn't ready to be a regular when I first joined Cleveland. I didn't have that kind of experience. But we had some great coaches who were fine teachers. I listened to what they told me and practiced. And I sat and watched Jim."

Kelly insisted he never tried to copy Jim, though there are many who feel he developed many mannerisms similar to Brown's, not only in his running style on the field, but also in his way of carrying himself, of dressing and of living off the field. After being tackled, he even got up slowly and limped back to the huddle slowly, seemingly in pain, exactly as Brown always did. Then he would explode again on the next play.

"It's not an act. It's a way of conserving your strength, of getting a rest," he explained. "There are even times when you try to go down soft instead of struggling for extra inches. There are times, too, it's worthwhile to kick and scratch for extra yardage. You get a feel for it, for the right times."

Kelly heard that Brown had retired to become an actor prior to the 1966 season. He admitted that his first reaction was, "Great! Now, maybe I'll get my chance." Then, he said, he began to doubt that Brown would stick to his retirement. But when the new season opened, Brown was not in uniform.

The bigger Ernie Green was shifted into Brown's fullback slot, and Kelly moved into Green's halfback position. Coach Collier was especially impressed by how hard the two worked to help each other. "I remember one play when Kelly ran 30 yards downfield to throw a beautiful block for Green," the coach recalled. However, Kelly soon assumed the star's role.

Of course Kelly wasn't asked to carry the ball as much as Brown had been. Jim had often carried the ball 30 to 35 times a game. Kelly usually carried only 15 or 20 times. But Kelly also was thrown passes a couple of times a game. In one respect he was Brown's equal—he was just as durable. Leroy missed only three plays in three seasons. In one game he dislocated a finger. He rushed to the sideline, had the trainer yank it back into place then ran right back onto the field, missing just one play.

Nick Skorich, the former offensive coach who replaced Collier after the 1970 season, said, "We came to see that if Kelly runs the ball close to 20 times a game, he'll gain 100 yards for us and break off a long one in that game sooner or later. He is not as big or strong as Brown, but he is quicker and just as tough." Whereas Brown was 6-foot-1 and 235 pounds, Kelly was 6-foot even and weighed 205 pounds.

Leroy proved his greatness when he finished second in NFL rushing in 1966 with 1,141 yards, first in 1967 with 1,205 yards and first again in 1968 with 1,239 yards. Each season he averaged five yards or more a carry, and he totalled 42 touchdowns.

Ernie Green said, "Leroy is like a cat. So was Jim Brown, only a bigger cat. It's difficult to knock a cat off his feet. Kelly is agile and has balance. Leroy doesn't have Jim's strength so he has to compensate in other ways. Jim broke tackles, Leroy slides through them. Leroy gives great fakes, sidesteps quickly and follows blockers brilliantly." A foe, Dick Bass, said, "Kelly has the quickest start of any runner ever. He also can change directions more sharply and at higher speed than any back I've ever seen."

Leroy got "off his marks" so swiftly that at first officials penalized him for "backfield in motion." But the Browns sent them films to study which showed that Kelly simply reacted to the snap of the ball swifter than others did. This enabled the small, tightly-muscled runner to explode into or around the line, behind blockers who were hard pressed to stay in front of him. Kelly even learned to stay a good distance behind his blockers so he didn't run over them.

The Browns always stressed good blocking. It is no accident they have had some of the best running records in recent years. "Running, like everything else, is as much a team effort as it is an individual thing," said Kelly. "That's why I don't pay much attention to statistics and titles. They have no value to me. All I'm interested in is our team winning the games. I'm proud of our winning record. I'm most

Green Bay Packer linebackers Dave Robinson (89) and Ray Nitschke (66) pursue a speedy Leroy Kelly.

disappointed we haven't made the Super Bowl or won the championship. That's my goal."

Kelly was unusually quiet and reserved. He seldom spoke unless spoken to and gave short answers to most questions. Over the years, even before he became a pro, his teammates spoke of how little he had to say, but they consistently noted that he remained a leader, one of those who leads by example, who inspires with his effort, and whose occasional comments have deep impact. "He makes the big play. He comes through when it counts," said Skorich.

Leroy Kelly gained sophistication with success. He lived in a plush, suburban bachelor apartment in Cleveland, well stocked with rock records and fancy clothes. He wore conservative cuts and conservative colors, but bought expensive tailor-made apparel. Once, he was selected by *Esquire* magazine as one of the ten "best-dressed young men" in America. He collected coins, fished and played a lot of golf. He always went his own way. Never close to Jim Brown while they were teammates, he became friendly with him after Brown retired. He worked for Brown's Negro Industrial Economic Union, which sought to set up blacks in business. He was active in civil rights causes, but in a quiet way.

When he and his brother Harold received bonuses for signing contracts in their respective sports, they promptly shared the down payment for a new home for their parents. Prior to the 1967 season Kelly refused to sign a contract with the Browns until they offered him more money. He played without a contract all that year, but just when it was rumored he might jump to another club, he agreed to a four-year contract for about $75,000 a season. "I never wanted to leave the Cleveland club. I did feel I should be paid what I felt I was worth," he commented.

As his value increased, he always was quick to point out he had been fortunate to escape injuries. Then in 1969's first game he pulled a leg muscle, and in 1970 he suffered two sprained ankles. His rushing records were reduced considerably. Even then, he said, "I'm fortunate not to have any broken bones or anything requiring operations. I'm lucky to have gone so long without being hurt. Many running backs have been hurt much more often and much more severely. It's a very risky business. I've been one of the lucky ones. If I'm fortunate, I'll be able to bounce back and run well for several years to come. But you can't count on anything in this business."

DICK BASS

·3·

ONCE, on a road-trip with the Los Angeles Rams, Dick Bass walked into the lobby of his hotel, wearing his typical super-fancy clothes—a homburg hat, an overcoat, a bright vest, and an umbrella hooked on one arm. Someone spotted him and asked, "Aren't you Bass of the Rams?" Bass drew himself erect in mock horror and said, "I, my good man, am Hobbes of Scotland Yard."

Another time, during pre-season practice, Bass finished a required mile run and announced, "Gentlemen, you have just seen the miracle mile. It is a miracle I finished. Under the circumstances, I feel that I did well. After all, I had a rather heavy load to carry. The coaches have been on my back all week."

Dick Bass was a fun-loving, quick-witted fellow. He also was one of the greatest high school, college and professional running backs in history. Yet he was somehow permitted to drift into retirement after the 1969 season without the fanfare he deserved.

Richard Lee Bass was born March 15, 1937, in Georgetown, Mississippi. His father often had to travel far away to support his family. He worked as a lumbermill hand in Chicago, as a cook in a Las Vegas night club and as a cement-finisher on Mare Island, California. In the middle 1940s he settled his family in Vallejo in northern California, where he worked at a magnesium plant and as a rigger and cable-splicer for a bridge-building company.

A one-time prize-fighter, all-around athlete and sports fan, Dick's father raised his two sons, Dick and Norman, Jr., to become athletes. He hung tires on trees in the backyard for them to throw baseballs and footballs through, put up a basketball hoop on the side of the garage for shooting practice, and even fashioned a pole-vaulting pit along the driveway. He risked his jobs, missing work to be at his sons' games. In 1950 his back was broken in an accident at work. He was in bed 21 days. Three days after he got out of bed, he hobbled to one of his sons' games on crutches.

"He pushed us, but it was what we wanted," Dick said. "He taught us fundamentals. If we would come home late at night, he would be very angry, unless we had been to a game. A game was the only acceptable excuse. He would take us to games. Mom went along with it. We lived and breathed sports."

The encouragement made a difference. Norman was a fine athlete in high school and college, and he pitched in the major leagues until he developed a sore arm. Later he played professional football as a defensive back.

Dick Bass gets ready for practice with the Los Angeles Rams in December of 1966.

Norman was good, but it was Dick who achieved stardom. He was a runner and jumper in track, a playmaking guard in basketball, a power-hitting catcher in baseball, and a breakaway runner in football. Dick was the first four-sport letterman in his high school's history.

The Bass family lived in a three-bedroom wooden house. Near them was a large mound of earth the kids called "Tank Hill." Every morning at six-thirty,

Dick ran up and down that hill. Other kids used it as a make-believe fort. Dick used it to toughen his legs, build up his chest, and gain strength and stamina.

He liked to play it "cool." He liked to have a reputation as "a swinger." He went to a lot of parties, but he usually sneaked home early so he could get his rest for the game the next day.

On the high school teams Dick did all the things boys dream of doing. His game-tying single and game-winning double won a prep all-star baseball game in San Francisco, qualifying him for an all-star baseball game at the Polo Grounds in New York. In that game he got the first hit, beat out a bunt, drew a walk, stole a base, and paced his team to victory.

But football was Dick's finest sport. He started in Hogan Junior High School when he was 14 years old. He stood only 5-foot-6 and weighed 145 pounds, but he was so swift and elusive that it was almost impossible for others his age to tackle him. He ran, returned punts and kickoffs, kicked extra points, passed and caught passes. In two seasons his team won 16 straight games. Dick scored 41 touchdowns, half of them on runs of 40 yards or more, and scored 246 points.

His reputation was so great that the stands were packed when he played his first game for Vallejo High School. Yet Dick did not start. Seven minutes into the game, he was given the ball for the first time and ran 69 yards for a touchdown. He was not given the ball again until the first play of the second half when he ran 55 yards before being pushed out of bounds on his foes' 30-yard-line. On the next play he gained 18 yards. Next he burst up the middle 12 yards and across the goal line.

Later he ran 52 yards and 73 yards for scores. He also made two long touchdown runs that were recalled on penalties. By then it was 28–7, and the coach mercifully withdrew his sophomore star. However, when Vallejo got the ball again, the fans clamored for Bass. Dick went back in with the ball on Vallejo's 41. He got the ball and scored, running 59 yards.

He wound up with 327 yards and five touchdowns in his first varsity game. In his first high school season Bass averaged almost 12 yards a carry. He totalled 1,726 yards, scored 31 touchdowns and 186 points. His team went undefeated in nine games, winning one game 82–0.

In his second season Dick was even better He averaged almost 15 yards a carry, totalled 1,964 yards, scored 37 touchdowns and 256 points. His team won all nine of its games, one of them by the score of 87–12.

In two seasons he was only once held to one touchdown in a game. Seven times he scored five touchdowns in a game, and once he scored six. He had 20 touchdowns cancelled by penalties, including one run of 93 yards and another of 100 yards. He probably was the greatest high school running back in history.

Almost every major football college in the country offered him scholarships. However, he did not have good grades and some colleges wanted him to go to junior college first. Others turned him off with high-pressure recruiting and promises of illegal money and gifts, which he feared might get him declared ineligible.

But Dick was impatient. He decided finally to attend College of the Pacific in nearby Stockton and try to be "a big fish in a little pond." To his surprise, he found many people were so disappointed he had not chosen a more glamorous college that they actually were angry with him. "Some friends stopped talking to me," he sighed.

Nevertheless, Dick enjoyed his time at Pacific. A jazz fan, he became a disc-jockey for a local radio station. He got married there and Dick's son, Ricki, was born.

As a freshman Dick scored 10 of his team's 11 touchdowns during a short schedule. Joining the varsity as a sophomore, he gained 611 yards and scored seven touchdowns for an ordinary team.

During Pacific's annual intrasquad exhibition game prior to his junior season, Bass was hit hard from the side. His right leg was bent unnaturally, tearing ligaments loose and breaking small bones in his ankle. Dick was taken to a hospital, and his ankle was operated on and repaired. He was out for the season. Then he re-broke the ankle sliding during the baseball season, requiring another operation and more inactivity. By the beginning of his fourth year of college there was worry that his injury might have hurt his future.

The season's opening game was in Berkeley against California, which had a powerful club that year and would eventually go to the Rose Bowl. On the opening series of plays Bass carried the ball 6, 3, 7, 15, and finally, 21 yards to score a touchdown. He then threw a pass for a two-point conversion and an 8–0 lead. Later he ran 31 yards for a touchdown, but this one was recalled on a penalty. Still later, he ran 78 yards through virtually the entire California team for a touchdown. Films later revealed that 10 different players got their hands on him but could not bring him down. He then threw another two-point pass.

But California was strong. They held a 20–16 lead with three minutes to go. Paced by Bass, Pacific drove to the California 23-yard-line. Bass took a pitchout at left end and ran down the sideline until bumped out of bounds at the one. Then the fullback scored. Bass then rolled out and passed for his third two-point conversion. Pacific won the game 24–20.

By season's end Dick led all collegians in the country in rushing with 1,361 yards, in total offense with 1,440 yards, and in scoring with 116 points. He was the first to win the NCAA "Triple Crown" in 30 years. His average of 6.6 yards per carry set an all-time NCAA record.

Because he missed one season sitting out with injuries, Dick still was eligible for one more year of college football. But he also was available for the pro draft. Every college player whose original college class is graduating is eligible. The Los Angeles Rams made Dick their first choice of the pro draft. He was the first junior ever chosen on the first round of the draft. The Rams would have to wait another year for him.

Dick Bass gets good blocking from his College of the Pacific teammates against Boston College in 1958.

Dick's last year in college was disappointing because he pulled a hamstring muscle in his left leg,
developed internal bleeding and blood clots, and
had to run in pain all season. Nevertheless, he gained
742 yards, averaging more than five yards a carry,
and scored eight touchdowns. He wound up his college career with 2,714 yards and 206 points. Com-
bined with his high school career, Bass had gained
6,404 yards and scored 101 touchdowns and 648
points in five seasons as an amateur. Now it was time
to turn professional.

When Dick joined the Rams in 1960, they were
one of the weakest teams in pro football. Their
coach, Bob Waterfield, did not believe in using
rookies regularly. Some of the team's coaches worried that Dick was too small to be effective among
the giants in pro ball. But one of the coaches, Hampton Pool, nicknamed Dick "The Little Motor
Scooter" and championed his cause. Nevertheless, in
his first pro year, Bass was used only sparingly as a
reserve halfback, end and kick-return specialist. He
gained 553 yards in total offense, and the team
finished with four victories in 12 games.

The NFL schedule was increased to 14 games the
next season and although the Rams won only four
games again, they did find a new star. Reluctant to
bench star halfback Jon Arnett, Pool suggested Bass
be tried at fullback. Although he was only 190
pounds, the tough little guy welcomed the opportunity. Bass explained, "I can't run over people, but I
can squirm through holes. In modern football, there
isn't a lot of difference between a halfback's duties

and a fullback's duties, except that a fullback runs inside more and blocks more, and I like to run in heavy traffic and I'm a good blocker."

Still, Bass did not get his first starting assignment until the sixth game of the season, in New York. In the third period the Giants led 10–7, and the Rams had the ball on their own 47. Bass took a pitchout, started to his right, ran into a swarm of tacklers, reversed his field, circled left, and picked his way through a broken field 53 yards to score. It was a dazzling display and the turning point in his pro career.

Against Green Bay he returned a kickoff 61 yards. In a rematch he returned a punt 90 yards and had a run from scrimmage of 55 yards. Against Minnesota he ran for 113 yards, including a 73-yard-run from scrimmage, the longest of the season in the NFL. By the end of the season he had rushed for 608 yards, averaging more than six yards a carry, and returned kicks and caught passes for 950 more yards.

In 1962 the Rams hit bottom with only one victory, but Bass reached the top by running for 1,033 yards from scrimmage and gaining 1,822 yards in total offense. In one game Bass ran for 140 yards and the other Ram backs ran for only 20 more. Detroit Lion coach George Wilson said, "That Bass has more movement than a fine watch. He is the greatest back we've had in the league in twenty years. You can beat the Rams, but I'm not sure you can beat this boy Bass."

Bass enjoyed playing, though he did not enjoy losing. He said, "All I can ever do is the best I can. I

Bass drives for a first down against the San Francisco
49ers in 1962.

expect to win every game we play. I mean that sincerely. I don't like losing. We do keep losing, but the morning of every game I wake up saying, 'This is our day,' and I play that way. I never give up."

Bass was a bit unorthodox. Once, being interviewed by a reporter, he suddenly burst into a frenzied dance, then stopped and answered a question. He dressed extravagantly, wore eyeglasses and did not look like a football player. Once he was stopped by a guard at the players' entrance. The guard said, "You're no football player." Bass looked at him haughtily and said, "I, my good man, am the football," and went in.

Bass said, "I like to have a good time. I'm Mr. Humor, fooling around. But when the time comes, I'm all business. This is a business, a tough business. There's a time and place for everything. I clown, but not in games on the field. Coaches worry about my attitude until they see that I keep in shape, practice hard and give games everything I have."

This was quite a bit. On the field he seemed dwarfed, but he was tough. He explained, "The first secret to success as a runner is to run as much as possible where there aren't any tacklers. This, very simply, involves finding the hole and getting through it quickly. Then you have to learn to follow any blocking help you can get. I learned from Hugh McElhenny, who was the smoothest runner I ever saw and one of the greatest at taking advantage of blocks. I run off the blocker's outside hip. I keep his body between me and the tackler.

"If I suddenly cut back, running right at the tacklers, running 'against the grain,' as it's called, I can often get right on by them because they can't stop and change directions quickly. I'm so short, they don't expect me to hit hard, but I'm 200 pounds and to their surprise they often find if they don't hit me hard, I hit them hard and burst right through their arms.

"If I'm going down, I'm going down. I relax. I never show I'm hurt or tired. Even when I'm roughed up, I never give a tackler any lip. If I say anything, it might be, 'Nice tackle,' or something like that. I make them think, 'That Richard Bass, what a sweet guy.' Maybe they won't feel so mean toward me next time and come at me quite as hard."

In 1963 Bass suffered a badly bruised heel that benched him two full games. In 1964 he suffered shoulder and knee injuries that kept him out of eight games. In 1965 he suffered a torn muscle in his right leg that knocked him out of three games. All those seasons the injuries handicapped him heavily in the games he could play. He was unable to run for much more than 500 yards in any of those years.

The team kept losing. In 1966 George Allen came in as new coach. Allen made many trades and pulled the Rams together. Also, Bass was able to get through the whole season healthy. Bass ran 248 times for 1,090 yards, setting new Ram records, and the team won more games than it lost for the first time in eight years. Dick was voted Ram MVP and All-Pro for the second time. He also was voted "Pro Football's Comeback Player of the Year." He said, "I've never been away, except when I was hurt. I never had help before. In the past, I was running for my life. This year, I was running for team titles."

In 1967 Allen worked to build up the team's passing game. He asked Bass to concentrate on his blocking while others ran more. Bass agreed to sacrifice himself. He ran for 627 yards, but blocked while others ran and passed for much more. Baltimore coach Don Shula said, "Bass gives passers as good protection as any back in the league." Ram coach Allen said, "Bass is one of the best blockers I've ever seen, and for his size he is the very best."

Bass said, "It's all technique. I have to block men much bigger than me, so the secret is to go out and hit them before they get in to hit me, hitting them before they get up their momentum, accepting punishment and staying with them as long as you can, giving your passer as much time as you can."

Many fans and friends sympathized with him for having a bad year. But Dick said, "You simply can't make people see that it is the team that counts, and if it is best for the team that I be run less and used more in other ways, I just have to do it." The team won its divisional pennant in 1967, but it was beaten in the championship playoff in Green Bay.

In a critical game that helped the Rams win the pennant, Bass fumbled once and dropped a touchdown pass and the fans started to boo him. But the team kept giving him the ball and in the end his runs as well as his blocks helped them win. In the dressing room later he said, "I did many things to help the team win which the fans didn't notice. They booed me. After all the good years I had when the team

was bad, this hurt. But that's football and that's life. You have to take the bad with the good. Now, all the writers and fans are around other players. They're the heroes. I'm just another player. But it's all right. I helped. And we won."

In 1968 Bass pulled a hamstring muscle in his left leg. He missed five games and was handicapped in the remaining five. He gained only 494 yards, and although the Rams had a winning record, they were beaten out for the divisional pennant.

In 1969 Dick injured his leg at the start of the season and was sidelined almost the whole year. He ran only one time for only one yard, and it was the last run and last yard of his career.

Few sad stories were written about him. No one seemed to notice as he stood in the shadows, wisecracking as usual with his teammates, but suddenly no longer an important part of the team. After ten seasons as a pro, he retired with team records of 1,218 runs and 5,417 yards gained. Yet there was no Dick Bass Day. No bands marched in his honor. After one of the greatest careers in football history— junior high school, high school, college and pro— Dick Bass departed quietly, with a smile. He took a coaching position at a small college and continued to live in his own, special, happy way.

Late in his career Bass takes a handoff from Ram quarterback Roman Gabriel (18).

O.J. SIMPSON

·4·

FOR TWO YEARS at the University of Southern California O.J. Simpson was the most publicized college football player in the country. Earlier stars like Red Grange, Tom Harmon and Glenn Davis never attracted the attention Simpson did because Simpson played in the era of television, when an entire nation could thrill to his talent.

O.J. carried the ball more often and gained more yards running than any collegian in history. Sprinter-fast, agile as a gymnast and tricky as a tumbler, he was a smooth, classic performer. He took his team through two tremendous seasons and to the Rose Bowl twice. He was voted not only All-America, but received the Heisman Trophy, which goes to only one college star each year. At the end of the 1960s he was named "Player of the Decade." Many considered him the outstanding college football runner of all time.

A reformed slum roughneck from San Francisco, Simpson was poised, personable, and extremely pleasant. He endured great pressure. On the field he was expected to produce miracles on cue. Off the field he was expected to surrender his time to writers and broadcasters. The fans followed him around, seeking autographs. Celebrities courted him. He gave of himself graciously to everyone. Only after it was over, did he admit, "It was the hardest time of my life. I hope I never have to go through anything like it again."

The pro football draft of college players is designed to keep the teams even in quality. Every year the team with the worst record gets the first pick of the graduating college stars. The players must either reach agreement with the team that drafts them or give up pro football. In 1969 the team with first choice was Buffalo, which had won only one game out of 14 during the previous season. As expected, the Bills chose O.J. Simpson.

Buffalo could not pay as much as other teams, nor support him with as much talent, but they had him. O.J. held out for a huge salary and reported to training camp late. When he arrived, he found that without big, skilled blockers, he could not run as effectively as he had in college. Although he had a fine season, he was considered a failure. His team won only four games. He returned in 1970 and was doing even better. Then he injured his knee and was sidelined the last part of the year. His team won only three games. Suddenly, he was in the shadows.

Even before he began his pro career, Simpson said, "I know that if I just become a real good pro, I'll be considered a bust. I won't be able to get by if

USC running star O. J. Simpson after being tackled in a game against Notre Dame in 1967.

I'm poor or ordinary and maybe not even if I'm just sort of outstanding. I've gotten so much publicity and I've asked so much money that if I'm not super-something, I'll be like nothing." After two seasons he sighed and said, "I thought the college pressure bad, but life as a pro has been worse. It's a harder game and I've had less chance to succeed in it. At least I got the job done in college. If life wasn't easy, at least I was on top. Here, life is not easy and

I'm on the bottom, trying to scratch my way up."

His handsome face seemed drawn. He had always been relaxed and smiling, but now he seemed tense and did not smile as easily. He was making a lot of money. He had a fine family and an expensive home. Yet he seemed somehow incomplete. "You make as much money as you can, but underneath it all, pride matters most," he said. "I'm a proud person. I'm proud of what I've accomplished in my life. It hasn't been easy. I'm proud of what I did in college. I'm not proud of my pro career yet.

"But those that are giving up on me are wrong," he continued. "My pro career has only just begun. My team is just now getting the sort of talent it needs to win. With help, I can become what everyone expected me to be. And I can help my team to win. I have not," he said, "come this far to give up now."

Orenthal James Simpson grew up in a black ghetto in San Francisco. He always used his initials because he would have been ridiculed for a name like Orenthal. His aunt had first discovered the name and had suggested it to O.J.'s mother; she stuck it on him and he has been stuck with it ever since. He also said, however, that using O.J. paid off because it was unusual and colorful and made him stand out over fellows named Bill or Tom. Naturally, he was nicknamed "Orange Juice," but to most it always was simply O.J.

As an infant, O.J. had a calcium deficiency, believed to be rickets. The deficiency left him with thin, bowed legs. He never had much when growing up. His parents separated when he was five and he was raised by his mother, who worked as a hospital orderly. He was a tough kid, often in trouble. He remembers stealing small things, starting fights, and being put in jail after a minor riot on the streets.

"I'm not proud of my past," he said. "I was lucky I didn't get into more trouble. I ran with a gang. Some of the guys I ran around with got hooked on narcotics or crime. If it hadn't been for football, that would've been me. I didn't know any better. And what could I have done? Dug ditches? I never even thought about going to college when I was a boy. I just thought about getting by somehow, any way I could. I'm the same person now I was then, only I got a chance to make it big by doing something straight and it settled me down. That's the big thing —the chance."

He was a standout on the football team at Galileo High School, which had mostly Oriental students and a small team. He got a chance to prepare for college at San Francisco City College, a junior college, and grabbed it. He was a sprinter in track and a sensational runner in football, rattling off a series of 80- and 90-yard runs and setting records for this level of competition. Sought by many schools, he selected USC simply because he "wanted to play for a winner." Ironically, he did not have such a choice when he entered pro ball.

At Southern Cal he followed in the footsteps of Mike Garrett, a Heisman Trophy winner who had set NCAA records by carrying the ball 612 times for

3,221 yards in 30 games over three seasons. Garrett averaged 20 carries and 106 yards a game. Simpson entered college ball as a junior, and few people suspected that he could surpass Garrett's performance or his records in only two years. However, as a junior Simpson ran 291 times for 1,543 yards, and as a senior he ran 383 times for 1,880 yards (setting a single-season collegiate record). He averaged 32 carries and 149 yards per game and set new NCAA marks of 674 carries and 3,423 yards rushed in his career. In short, he did more in two years than Garrett had done in three.

As usual, statistics tell only a small part of the story. Simpson proved to be a pressure performer who did his best when it counted the most. In his first game against national power Notre Dame, which had humiliated USC 51–0 the season before, O.J. scored three touchdowns in the second half to rally the Trojans to a stirring come-from-behind triumph. In his first game against arch-rival UCLA he ran 64 yards for a touchdown late in the contest to bring USC a 21–20 victory and an invitation to the Rose Bowl. The following year he led USC back to the Rose Bowl by scoring three touchdowns in a 28–16 conquest of UCLA. In the 1967 Rose Bowl Purdue defeated the Trojans 14–13. But in 1968 Simpson foiled the defenses of Indiana and brought USC a 14–3 victory to revenge the earlier loss to Purdue.

Simpson was used so often as a workhorse that fans and press sympathized with him, prompting USC coach John McKay to point out, "He doesn't

Simpson sails in for the score against Indiana during the 1968
Rose Bowl.

belong to a union. He'll run as often as we need him to run. The more he runs, the better he gets, you know," McKay added.

Simpson agreed: "When I get tired, I stop thinking so much and run more naturally and do better. Oh man, but I would get tired. The bumps and bruises would really begin to hurt the night after a game. My wife and I would go out to a party or a movie and I'd try to stretch it out because I wouldn't want to go home. I'd go home, I'd sit up half the night watching TV because I didn't want to go to bed. Because when I'd get in bed, I couldn't sleep. Mental tension. And just plain physical pain. Every way I'd turn, every place I'd lay, I'd hurt. The next day would be awful.

"I played with injuries. You've got to. My first year in college a teammate stepped on my foot and my arch got ripped up. My second year I got a bruised thigh, a twisted knee and a sort of cramp in my calf. I couldn't practice. But, come the games, I could always play.

"People used to kid me about laying so long, like dead, after being tackled, and then getting up so slowly and going back to the huddle so slowly, but I had to to get all the rest I could get. I told my quarterback sometimes when I was too tired to run. Once I did and he called a pass play and I was relieved. But when he got to the line and saw the defense, he switched to another run by me and I ran 64 for a score. I could always find it in me to turn it loose just one more time."

That may have been his greatest run. It came late

in his first USC-UCLA game. Simpson had already picked up a 13-yard touchdown run to give USC a 14–7 halftime lead. But UCLA rallied and led 20–14 with time running out. USC seemed stalled with third down and eight yards to go on its own 36-yard-line: a passing situation. Quarterback Steve Sogge called for a pass, then changed the call to a run at the line of scrimmage. Simpson took the hand-off, shot through a hole on the right side and veered to the left. Suddenly he cut sharply back to the right, throwing defenders off balance, and sprinted into the end zone.

It was simply stunning. One coach said, "That was the best single run I ever saw. He made a 90-degree cut without losing a step, which no man ever has done. I haven't seen all the fine runners, but he's the finest I've ever seen." UCLA coach Tommy Prothro said, "I'm deeply disappointed to lose, but when you lose to a super-run by a super-star like that one, you have to accept the inevitable."

After such heroics Simpson was frustrated by his lack of opportunities in his first year at Buffalo. The Bills had the smallest and least effective blocking linemen in the league. They fell behind early in most games, so they passed more and more as the games went on. O.J. averaged only 13 carries a contest, and when he did run, he found little room.

The Bills did not seem to realize that stamina and strength were among his strongest points. He had a slender build for a running back—6-foot-2 and 197 pounds—and he was fast, once sprinting 100 yards in only 9.4 seconds. Yet he actually had few long

Returning a kickoff for Buffalo, Simpson breaks a tackle by
Raider Howie Williams.

runs in college. Instead, he seemed to wear his foes down. He carried the ball over and over. As the game went on, his foes got weaker and he got stronger. He piled up most of his yardage in the last parts of his games. At Buffalo he never had a chance to wear down an opponent.

Still, he gained 697 yards to place sixth in the AFL. In 181 rushes he averaged just under four yards a carry. He gained 343 yards on 30 pass-catches, and 529 yards on 29 kickoff returns, averaging more than 25 yards a runback. His total offense of 1,570 yards was tremendous. Yet few seemed to notice. In fact, a Boston rookie, Carl Garrett, with less impressive statistics, was voted Rookie of the Year. O.J. had been right when he suggested that if he didn't lead the league in everything right away, he was bound to be labelled a flop.

In 1970 a similar situation was developing before he was injured. He was averaging only 15 carries a game, though still running with passes and kickoffs spectacularly. He was averaging more than four yards a carry and had carried 120 times for 488 yards, third best in the league at that point, when he injured his left knee during the eighth game of the season. He was sidelined the rest of the way. And again he was considered a disappointment.

Those who watched the game closely had a different opinion, however. San Diego coach Sid Gillman said, "Will he make it? O.J. made it the day he was born. He was born to run. It's just a shame he has to be with that team." New York Jet linebacker Larry Grantham said, "O.J. has the potential to be the best back who ever ran. He only needs more help." Buffalo coach John Rauch said, "Even if it hasn't shown in our record yet, we're improving rapidly. So is O.J. As we give him more help, his greatness will come out again."

Simpson was touched by Floyd Little's thoughtfulness during the season. "He saw I was disappointed. He sought me out to tell me not to get discouraged. He said he'd had a great college career, but had gotten nowhere in his first couple of years as a pro, which is true."

Off-seasons Simpson still was settled in Los Angeles, living with his wife, Marguerite, and two young children in a luxurious house he had built in a wealthy suburb. He was leading the good life. Yet he was dissatisfied. "Image is a big thing with me," he confessed. "I was recognized as the best at one time and I want that again.

"I've done better than most persons realize," he concluded. "But I have to do a lot better yet. When I do, my team will do better. No one lives alone in this life. And no one plays football alone. I am determined that O.J. will be Number One again. But I will not be satisfied until I help a team to the top again. When we win, I win. It takes time. Nothing worthwhile in life comes easy. If I didn't know that before, I do now."

THE BREAKAWAY ARTISTS

GALE SAYERS   MEL FARR   DICK POST
MIKE GARRETT   DONNY ANDERSON   MacARTHUR LANE

· 5 ·

LATE IN THE 1968 season Gale Sayers, thought by many to be the greatest running back in pro football, tried to make a sharp cut around Kermit Alexander of the San Francisco 49ers. Just as Sayers dug his right foot into the turf, Alexander rolled into him. His cleats caught and under the force of the blow, Sayers' knee bent sideways. Sayers rolled on the ground in agony, screaming, "It's gone, it's gone."

He tried to get up to test it, but the knee buckled under him and he went down again. A doctor rushed on field to examine him. Sayers moaned, "It's gone, doc."

The doctor said, "It's O.K."

"Tell me the truth," Sayers demanded angrily.

The doctor shrugged and said, "It's gone."

Gale was helped to the sidelines. There he put his head in his hands and began to cry. He kept asking himself, he said later, "Why me? Why did it have to happen to me?"

Thus in the fourth year of his pro career a cloud

was cast over Sayers that never completely lifted. He was born on Memorial Day 1940 in Wichita, Kansas. Later his family moved to a place called Speed, Kansas, and then to Omaha, Nebraska. Gale's father was a farmer, an auto repairman and finally a car-polisher in a used-car lot. He worked very hard for very little.

Gale remembered moving nine times in eight years within Omaha's black belt. He remembered many meals of chicken feet, which could be bought 100 for 50 cents. He remembered his parents drinking and being unhappy because of their lot in life. Gale said he was inspired to somehow do better and have more. He never smoked or drank and practiced hard for success in sports. Sports were for him, as for many poor boys, a way out of poverty and unhappiness.

Gale's older brother, Win, was a fine football player and track performer. So was his younger brother, Ron, who followed Gale into the NFL. But Gale was the athletic star of the family. In high school he shone in four sports. He excelled in baseball and basketball. He was a record-setting long-jumper and a fine sprinter and hurdler. But he was best at football. He had unique ball-carrying ability. He was quick and shifty and was able to make the sharpest cuts at top speed without losing a step. He won high school All-America honors.

At Kansas University he won collegiate All-America laurels. He totalled 2,675 yards and averaged more than six yards a carry. A 6-foot, 200-pounder, he was not the big workhorse of a runner that pro

The Chicago Bears' star halfback, Gale Sayers, runs with swashbuckling style to cut past New York Giant defenders.

teams are always seeking, but his ability to make the big breakaway run attracted them. He was taken in the first rounds of the pro drafts by Kansas City of the AFL and Chicago of the NFL, and signed with Chicago.

He earned Rookie of the Year honors in 1965, finishing second in rushing in the NFL with 867 yards and setting a new league record with 22 touchdowns. In one game, against San Francisco, he ran only nine times, but gained 336 yards and scored six times, tying another league mark.

The following season he led the NFL in rushing with 1,231 yards, and gained 762 yards on kick returns and 447 yards on pass receptions to set a new one-season NFL standard for total offense with 2,440 yards. In 1967 he slipped to 880 yards rushing, but gained 603 yards more on kick returns.

Chicago had only ordinary teams in these years. Its passing game was poor and Sayers' running ability was most of the team's offense. He made as many spectacular runs as any man in the history of professional football, many of them covering 80 yards or more. He set a league record with six touchdowns on kickoff returns, these covering 90, 93, 96, 97, 97 and 103 yards. Long-time foe Deacon Jones said, "You reach for him and he's gone. No one ever could change directions, shift speeds, accelerate and go like him."

When the NFL selected an all-time all-star team to celebrate its golden anniversary, Jim Brown and Gale Sayers were named the running backs. In Sayers' case, it was a rare honor for one so young and so inexperienced. Then, in 1968, he was far ahead of league rushers with 856 yards and had 461 yards in kickoff returns when he was injured in the ninth game. Every ligament in his knee was torn. He was on the operating table three hours. Later, he had to endure an ordeal of painful exercises to rebuild his leg. Yet he made an awesome comeback in 1969, winning his second league rushing championship with 1,032 yards. In 1970, however, he suffered an injury to his other knee early in the season and had to undergo yet another serious operation.

Reserved almost to the point of being a recluse, Sayers lived quietly with his wife, daughter and adopted son. His flashiness was reserved for the football field. After just six seasons as a professional, however, his colorful career was in deep danger of being prematurely curtailed.

In Mel Farr's first game with the Detroit Lions he broke his nose. In his second he broke it again. In his third he broke his toe. But he wore plastic protective devices and kept going. He rushed for 860 yards, caught passes for 317 yards, and was voted Rookie of the Year in the NFL for 1967. But his troubles were just beginning.

Midway in his second season he was leading the league in rushing when he injured his knee and missed the final five games. Early in his third season he re-injured his knee and missed the last 10 games. In his fourth season, 1970, he established himself as one of the best by rushing for 717 yards, but separated his shoulder late in the campaign. He continued playing with his shoulder protected by a special harness, but he was ineffective.

Farr, born in November of 1943 in Beaumont, Texas, certainly came from a football family. His older brother, Miller, and a cousin, Clancy Williams, became top pro defensive backs, while another cousin, Jerry LeVias, despite small size, became a spectacular clutch runner and receiver in pro ranks. Mel earned All-America honors on potent UCLA teams and was drafted first by the Detroit Lions. Then his battle with injuries began.

A 6-foot-2, 200 pounder, he described himself as more of a slashing runner than a shifty one. When healthy, he was featured in one of the fine running backfields in football. It included stocky Altie Taylor, who ran for 666 yards in his second season in 1970, and rangy quarterback Greg Landry, who ran for 350 yards.

Steve Owens, the 1969 Heisman Trophy winner as the outstanding college football player in the country, had surpassed O.J. Simpson's college record by gaining 3,867 yards during his career at Oklahoma. But he could not break into the regular Lion backfield. Like Farr, he was learning that even the most talented players often had to face many disappointments before they could achieve real stardom in this game.

No one understood this better than Donny Anderson, who came out of Texas Tech as one of the most highly-regarded pro prospects ever. He signed a long-term $600,000 bonus contract with the Green Bay Packers, which startled the sporting public, then

A lucky stab catches Mel Farr's shoe and sends the Detroit
Lion running back flying.

floundered through five pro years seeking to establish himself.

Born in May of 1943 in Borger, Texas, Donny was a small-school All-State linebacker in high school who became a brilliant all-around back in college. At 6-foot-3 and 220 pounds, he did everything well and was not even considered a running specialist. Still, he was notoriously inconsistent. A handsome blonde, he was considered a "swinger" and was nicknamed "Cocky."

At Green Bay Anderson followed in the footsteps of another handsome, cocky, blonde swinger, Paul Hornung. Hornung had never run for great yardage, but he had been tough near the goal line and had developed a great following among football fans. He was called "The Golden Boy." Anderson was called "The New Golden Boy."

However, Anderson rode the bench most of his early pro career. He became a regular only in his third season and rushed for 761 yards, but was benched again through his fourth season. Then he came back in 1970 with 853 yards. Finally, he may have found his way.

Mike Garrett had a fine pro career, but he was another who never quite lived up to his college reputation. He had set the NCAA career record for rushing (later broken by O.J. Simpson and Steve Owens) with 3,220 yards. He, too, won the Heisman Trophy.

At 5-foot-9, 195 pounds, Garrett was small, but he was strong and quick, an exciting "jitterbug" sort of runner. Garrett turned pro with Kansas City of the

AFL and ran for 801 yards as a rookie and 1,067 yards as a second-year man. In the next two seasons he slipped to 564 yards and 732 yards because he was troubled by injuries.

Born into a broken family in April of 1944 in Los Angeles, brought up in a depressed area, he was another who found football a way out of poverty. But unlike many players, he was never in love with the sport. He admitted, "I sort of shake like a leaf in the wind as games approach.

"People say football players are overpaid," he said, "but I ask them if they ever had to crawl to the bathroom as I literally have had to do the morning after some games. Sometimes I get hit so hard in games that I lie on the ground and wonder why I'm doing this. For the money, I guess. And you have to accept getting kicked and knocked down and run over all through life. But it's like you're in a dark alley and you're running from trouble and you know you can get hurt if you get caught, so you keep running."

"I'm not chicken because I keep going back in that alley," he concluded.

In 1970 Garrett made plans to give up football in favor of baseball. But then he was traded to San Diego and decided to stick to the sport in which he was established.

On the Chargers Garrett joined another tiny but spectacular runner, 5-foot-9, 185-pound Dick Post. "I've been the smallest man on the field wherever I played and I always did all right so I never think about my size," he said.

Post was born in San Pedro, California, in September of 1945, but grew up in the towns of Seminole, Hominey, Bartlesville, Pawhuska and Pauls Valley in Oklahoma, where his stepfather worked in the oil fields. Dick played college football at the University of Houston, where he was sixth in the nation in rushing in 1966 with 1,061 yards, but was overshadowed in Houston by teammate Warren McVea.

Post was picked by San Diego in the fourth round. The Chargers planned to make him a wide receiver, but when injuries sidelined Paul Lowe, a regular Charger running back, Dick took over. Soon afterward, Lowe retired.

On his first pro play Post was slammed down by Houston's 6-foot-9, 320-pound Ernie Ladd. But Dick bounced right back up and did so well the rest of the game that Ladd sought him out afterward, stuck out his huge hand and said, "Little man, you're gonna' be a fine football player."

Post fulfilled the prophecy. Nicknamed "Scooter," he ran for 663 yards in 1967, his rookie year. In his second year he ran for 758 yards and led the league with an average of more than five yards a carry. In 1969 he led the league again with 873 yards.

However, Post had to have knee operations after each of his first two seasons. Then he hurt his knee again and had to have another knee operation just prior to his fourth season, 1970. Just six weeks later he was back with the team and running brilliantly. But then he hurt his shoulder. He played with the injury but had another operation after the season.

A handsome, mod young man, who operated a

Mike Garrett kicks up the dirt in an effort to escape the grasping hand at his neck.

couple of mod clothing stores in the San Diego area, Post was, along with Donny Anderson and Larry Csonka, among the few outstanding white runners in a specialty that has been dominated by blacks. Quick, tricky and tough, he continued to battle injuries in his drive to the top.

"He'll come back," Charger publicist Jerry Wynn predicted. "Everyone gets hurt in this game. The coaches look for the kids who play with injuries. That's Dick Post."

The threat of injuries made many running backs

San Diego Charger running back Dick Post dances his way downfield.

try even harder to succeed while they had the chance. One of these was MacArthur Lane, who first gained wide attention in the 1970 season with the Cardinals.

"No one gets hit harder and more often than a running back," Lane pointed out. "I figure a running back has maybe three, four years to do his thing. More than that, he's just plain lucky. I hit the top late. I'm no kid. I'd like to quit on top, when I can walk out, before I'm crippled and have to limp away, so I'm in a hurry to do big things fast."

Lane was the third-best rusher in pro football in

1970, gaining 977 yards. He ranked only behind Larry Brown (1,125 yards) and Ron Johnson (1,027 yards). But statistics do not tell the whole story. Lane was an unusually versatile player. During his college career he played quarterback and linebacker as well as running back. He was also the emergency punter and place-kicker for the Cardinals. And if the offensive center had been hurt, Lane would have gone in and snapped the ball back to the punter or field goal kicker.

MacArthur Lane was born in Montgomery, Alabama, on March 16th, 1942. He was named after Army General Douglas MacArthur. Lane's father was a construction worker. When MacArthur was three, his father moved his family to Alameda, California, where he took a job in the shipyards. Later the family moved to near-by Oakland.

Lane remembered his early training for sports. He recalled: "Growing up, we played all those agility games that kids love, but grownups seem to forget— walking the railroad tracks, diving off bridges, climbing up the sides of new buildings, dodging traffic. I matured quick and had the advantage of size. In the 12th grade I was 5-foot-11 and 195 pounds. When we played tackle in the parks and vacant lots, none of the kids could take me down."

Lane won All-City honors at Fremont High School, where he played quarterback as well as running back. After high school he went to work as a machinist's apprentice, operating a lathe in a factory. But MacArthur wanted to play football. He saved some money and enrolled at Merritt Junior

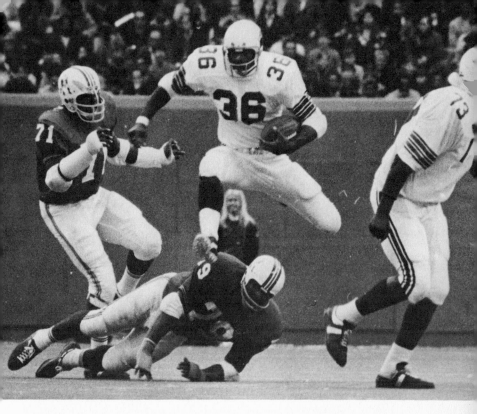

MacArthur Lane hurdles a downed Boston Patriot tackler.

College, where he won Junior College All-America honors and a scholarship to Utah State.

At Utah State he was a linebacker until midway in his junior year when he was converted to running back. He carried the ball 66 times, gained 662 yards and averaged 10 yards a carry the rest of the season. As a senior, he carried 96 times, gained 627 yards and averaged six yards a run until injured and sidelined the last part of the season.

Because of Lane's great potential, the Cardinals drafted him early. However, he injured his knee just before the start of his first season, in 1968. He later ruptured an artery in his left hand, which made it difficult for him to handle the ball. Then he tore ligaments in his right knee in 1969. Those two seasons he ran from scrimmage only 48 times and gained only 167 yards. His longest run was 13 yards. However, in 1969 he did return kickoffs 523 yards, averaging 26 yards a try.

Lane finally received his chance in 1970 and proved he was tough. In one game, against Philadelphia, he scored four times. He also had a 75-yard run which was stopped before he scored the touchdown. In his best game he gained 146 yards in 28 attempts against Washington, the best single-game performance of the year in the NFC. Although the Cardinals finished disappointingly, Lane had made his name and many considered him the outstanding "discovery" of the season.

A mod dresser who favored such clothes as buckskin jackets and bell-bottom trousers, Lane also wore a "Fu Manchu" mustache and a wispy goatee. Yet he was a strong family man. He and his wife, Edna, had one child of their own and adopted Edna's brother and sister when the children's mother died.

"If you can afford it, you gotta' help out," he said. "As a pro football player, I can afford it."

He liked to hunt and fish, and in the future he hoped to operate a pet shop or a tropical fish store. For the moment, however, football was his business and pleasure. He was not the first who had waited for fame, but having found it in one explosive season, he ranked as one of the most promising performers of the 1970s.

THE WORKHORSES

**JIM NANCE   LARRY CSONKA   JIM KIICK
HEWRITT DIXON   KEN WILLARD   MATT SNELL**

· 6 ·

THE SHOULDERS OF JIM NANCE seemed to stretch from sideline to sideline. His chest seemed to extend into the far end zone. He was built like a barrel—with legs. He was 6-foot-1, but seemed short because he was so wide. As a pro fullback his weight varied from 230 to 265 pounds. He had an enormous appetite for everything from 20-pound lobsters to chocolate cream pies. He was a pure fullback who could not outrun foes, but could power right through them. But the weight he carried may have excessively burdened his ankles. They gave way, threatening an early end to his career.

There are two distinct types of running backs in football: the small, quick fellows like Floyd Little and Dick Post, and the big, strong guys like Jim Nance and Ken Willard. The halfbacks in pro ball seem to get bigger every season, but the fullbacks are bigger yet. Although their assignments seem to get more similar each year, the fullback remains the heavy-duty inside runner, and the big backfield blocker. In contrast with the flashy specialist, such as kick-returner Alvin Haymond, the fullback is a workhorse.

Since Bronko Nagurski, football has been typified by the large, tough, fearless fullbacks who carried the ball right into the pit, who did not elude danger, but defied it. Perhaps the best of the modern fullbacks was Jim Taylor, who in his prime was the dynamite of the Green Bay Packers. Jim Brown was better, but was as swift as he was strong and ran more like a halfback than a fullback. The burly Taylor smashed and scratched and elbowed to 1,000 yards or more five different seasons. His one-season high of 1,307 yards and his 10-year totals of 1,941 carries, 8,597 yards and 83 touchdowns on the ground have been exceeded only by Brown.

Nance became the best fullback in the 10-year history of the AFL. He won two straight AFL rushing titles with a league-record 1,458 yards in 1966 and 1,216 yards in 1967. He set league records with 38 carries in a game and 299 in one season. He had more 100-yard games in a season, eight, and a career, 17, than any player ever. By 1970, his sixth season in pro ranks, he had run for 4,860 yards.

Nance was born in December, 1942, in Indiana, Pennsylvania, one of 10 children. His father was a coal miner. When Nance was an infant, he accidentally was scalded by boiling water. He was hospitalized 77 days and was permanently scarred on his left side. When a boy was killed playing football on a field next to the Nance home, Jim's father forbade him to play the game. But he began playing in the

Big Jim Nance of the Boston Patriots bulls his way forward
despite two persistent Houston tacklers.

seventh grade, and by the time his father found out, Jim was too good to be denied.

A high school football and wrestling star, he became a football standout and NCAA heavyweight wrestling champion at Syracuse University, where he was hailed as "the new Jimmy Brown." He followed Brown and Ernie Davis and preceded Floyd Little there, but he was inconsistent and fell short of the records established by his predecessors. He said, "I knew I was no Brown and got tied up in knots trying to be like him. And I was halfway through my first year as a pro before I realized even a guy my size needs a little running room to build up momentum."

Nance reported to Boston of the AFL so overweight that the coach threatened to make him a lineman. Throughout his career he went on crash diets and starved himself at times to stay within reasonable proportions. Still, he worked hard and unselfishly, and his Patriot coach once said, "Big Bo is the most popular player ever on this club." Commenting on his bruising running style, the Boston trainer said, "The contact in this game ruins all runners, and Nance doesn't have contact, he has collisions."

By the early 1970s wear and tear and ankle problems slowed Nance down, and big Larry Csonka of Miami emerged as the AFC's premier fullback. Born in Stow, Ohio, on Christmas Day, 1946, Csonka grew up on a farm and worked hard. He developed late, but big. He was a lineman during part of his high school career. He later became a runner, but won no honors. However, Syracuse scouts were impressed by his size and potential and he became yet another super runner there.

Csonka, a 6-foot-3, 235-pounder, broke all the records of the immortals who preceded him at the upstate New York university. He had 43 carries and 216 yards in one game, 1,127 yards in one season and 597 carries and 2,934 yards in three seasons. Coach Ben Schwartzwalder, who developed Brown, Davis, Little and Nance before Csonka, said, "Larry did more with less support than the others. He was the most valuable individual player I've coached."

Pro scouts worried about Csonka's lack of speed, but Miami picked him on the first round. When he reported heavy, he was placed at "the fat man's table," where overweight players were put on a diet. He lost a few pounds and slowly established himself as a pro standout. Despite severe injuries, he gained 540 yards his first season, 566 his second, and 874 his third, 1970.

Csonka took a lot of punishment. Once, when hurt, he refused a stretcher and insisted on walking off the field. He had to get a special protective helmet to go on playing after suffering two severe brain concussions. Doctors hinted that perhaps he should retire.

He was of Hungarian descent and his name was pronounced "Chunka" in the old country and "Sahn-ka" in this country. His teammates called him "Zonk" and he was nicknamed "Zonk the Bronc." He liked it so much he accepted "Zonk-ah" as correct. He said, "Zonk sounds like the kind of football

Miami Dolphin Larry Csonka carries the ball for 12 yards
against the St. Louis Cardinals.

player I am. Not exciting. There's not much excitement in four yards and a cloud of dust. But that's
me.

"I like to get dirty," he commented. "It's good to
feel dirt and blood on you. It makes you feel like a
football player. That's what football is all about. I'm
a very basic guy."

Csonka and his teammate at Miami, 5-foot-11,
220-pound Jim Kiick, formed the largest running

pair in pro ball. Born in Paterson, New Jersey, in August of 1946, the chunky Kiick grew up in Lincoln Park and developed into a solid, though unspectacular football player at Wyoming. Drafted fifth the same year Csonka was drafted first, the smaller but swifter Kiick outshone his running mate for two seasons before Csonka asserted himself in 1970.

In his first three seasons as a pro, the agile Kiick ran for 1,854 yards and caught passes for 1,362 yards. Being big does not prevent a fellow from being hurt, as Nance and Csonka would attest. But Kiick was unusually durable, playing and carrying the ball every game of his first three seasons, fumbling only once or twice a season. He had longer runs than Csonka, and while both were good blockers, Kiick was the better of the two.

Kiick was a halfback who ran like a fullback. Another such running back was Hewritt Dixon, a 6-foot-1, 230-pounder, who helped Oakland to four divisional pennants and one AFL league championship between 1966 and 1970. Raider boss Al Davis said, "We have had no more valuable player."

Dixon was born in January of 1940 in LeCross, Florida, and grew up in Alachua, a farmtown, where he worked in the fields with his brothers and sisters. There was one school for all grades, and boys were permitted to play high school varsity ball as soon as they were good enough. As a 12-year-old sixth-grader, Hewritt weighed 202 pounds and beat out his 18-year-old uncle for a starting tackle job. Later he became a running back.

He attended Florida A&M, where he was the

slowest man in a backfield although he could run the 100-yard dash in 9.9 seconds. He was thus nick-named "Freight Train," became a blocking back and was overshadowed by sprint champion Bob Hayes. He was drafted by Denver of the AFL in the eighth round, and with the Broncos he became a tight end of only modest attainments. After his third pro year he was traded to Oakland.

The Raiders had a fine runner, Clem Daniels, who wound up his career in 1967 with AFL records of 1,134 carries and 5,101 yards. Dixon was tried at running back and took over. He ran and caught passes for considerable yardage every season despite knee and shoulder injuries. He killed the pain with pills to keep playing, and then was repaired in off-season operations.

His big years were 1968, when he rushed for 187 yards in one game and 865 in the season and caught passes for 360 yards; and 1970, when he ran for 861 yards and caught passes for 207 yards. His running partner, Charlie Smith, ran for 681 yards in 1970 and they were the most effective duo in the conference.

If fellows like Mike Garrett and Dick Post had been boxers, they would have had to handle heavy-weights. But they were small by pro football stand-ards. They had to outmaneuver defenses. On the other hand, fellows like Dixon and the 6-foot-3, 225-pound Matt Snell did not give away much height and weight to most defenders. They could

Hewritt Dixon is flipped sideways and headed for a fall during
the 1968 Super Bowl against Green Bay.

smash right through tackles if necessary. Snell was all fullback. He did not make the flashy long runs, but he made the tough, short ones. "I just lower my head and go," he said.

Snell was born in August of 1941 in Garfield, Georgia, but later moved to New York. He was recruited by Ohio State and became the best of many fullbacks who played on Woody Hayes' "Four Yards and a Cloud of Dust" offense. He was drafted in the first round by the New York Jets and in his first season ran for 948 yards and caught passes for 393 yards, winning Rookie of the Year laurels for 1964.

Except for one year when he was laid out by a knee injury, Snell gained 600 to 800 yards for several seasons after that. In the playoffs following the 1968 season, he tore into Oakland 19 times for 71 yards to help the Jets win the AFL title game 27–23. Then, against Baltimore in the Super Bowl, he ran for 123 yards in 21 carries and gained 40 yards on four catches in the Jets' dramatic 16–7 triumph. Joe Namath emerged as the hero, but it was Snell who carried the ball over for New York's lone touchdown in that classic.

In 1969 Snell ran for 695 yards, but in 1970 he was sidelined by an injury. By then, the ranking fullback in pro football probably was another veteran, Ken Willard. In six pro seasons through 1970 he ground out 778, 763, 510, 967, 557 and 789 yards. He was seldom praised, but was consistently effective.

Willard was born in July of 1943 in Richmond, Virginia. When he was 14, his father died and his

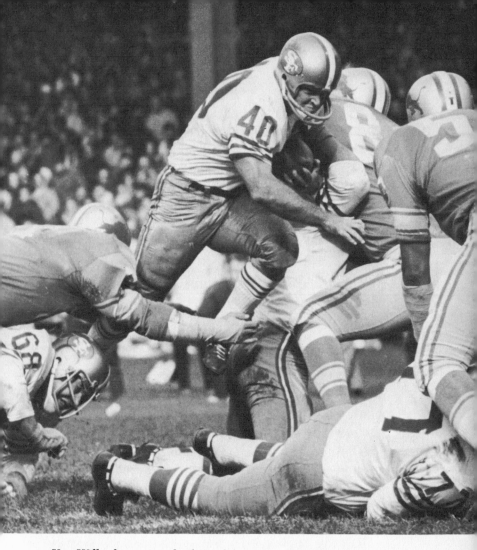

Ken Willard sneers in the face of threatening Detroit Lion tacklers.

mother had a hard time raising her family. Yet she insisted on her sons getting as much schooling as possible. Ken, who won 16 letters in four sports in high school, turned down a $100,000 baseball bonus offer extended to him by Ted Williams on behalf of the Boston Red Sox. Instead, he attended the University of North Carolina, where he was an honors student as well as an All-America football player.

Drafted in the first round in 1965 by San Francisco, Willard quickly became the Bay Area bull. He performed heroically for a series of disappointing 49er teams, then helped them to their first conference championship in 1970. Willard carried the ball 40 times for 127 yards in his team's two playoff games.

Former coach Jack Christiansen said, "Few players in football have been as underrated. He resists and shakes off injuries and does a dirty job well game after game."

The articulate Willard said, "Perhaps if I had gained 1,000 yards in a season or won a league rushing title, I'd have become better known, but I have mainly been consistent from year to year. I make few long runs people will remember. Few people realize how much yardage I'm gaining until it's added up later. I thrive on work. I get tired, but so do the defenders.

"I'm not the best blocking back in football, but I'm better than most. Springing another runner free gives me as much satisfaction as going on a good run myself. I take pride in my all-around performance."

At 6-foot-2 and 230 pounds, Willard was an ideal fullback. Smaller men, such as 5-foot-10, 200-pound Dick Bass of Los Angeles, have made fine fullbacks, but most have been large. They were not as flashy or as publicized as some running backs, but they were the ones asked to gain the hard yards, the yards that gained victories for their teams.

ALVIN HAYMOND

·7·

ALVIN HAYMOND was a specialist. He ran back punts and kickoffs. He also played defensive back and on the special kick-coverage teams, but he earned his living primarily by returning kicks. Unlike the heavy-duty fullback, who would carry the ball 25 or 30 times a game, Haymond ran with it only four times a game on the average.

Yet, many times Haymond gained more yardage than any other runner in a game. If he did not score, he often set up more scores than any other runner. Often he was the most spectacular performer in a contest.

Also, he was often hit harder and punished more severely than any player on either side. In seven years as a pro, Haymond had his front teeth knocked out, had his shoulder dislocated several times and was knocked unconscious countless times.

He was small by pro standards, which was proba-bly the reason he had not become a regular running back. But he was rugged. He had to be. The kick-return specialist is virtually helpless as he waits under a punt. The opposition's fastest and most fearless tacklers bear down on the kick-returner, hoping to slam into him the instant he catches the ball. He has blockers, but it is difficult to block kick-coverage men in an open field. If things are tight, he can call for a "fair catch" and give up the runback. Alvin Haymond called for fewer fair catches than any other specialist in recent seasons.

"I always say if they want somebody back there to 'fair-catch' 'em, they'll pick an end. Ends have better hands than me," he once said. "They put me back there because I can get 'em yards on kicks. Even one yard is better than none. It would be no good if I fumbled much when hit immediately, but I seldom fumble.

"There's no such thing as not being afraid. You know the tacklers are there, waiting to cream you. But you wipe this out of your mind by concentrating day after day on nothing more than catching the ball. In practice, I field maybe 50 punts a day. I want them spiralling, end over end, wobbling, sailing, every which way, so I learn to adjust and handle 'em. Drop one and the other side takes over in scoring position. So, it's pressure.

"You feel it when those linemen are coming down on you, but you have to think of catching the ball first. If there's another back with you, he may study the defenders moving in and signal to me if a fair catch is the only way out. Otherwise, I make my own decision. If it's hopeless, O.K. Otherwise, I'll take the chance and try to get away.

"Sometimes you fool 'em. I can usually beat off the first guy with a stiff-arm or forearm. It's the second guy that tries to kill you. Get away from him and you can go. Sometimes a sudden change of direction will do the job. Or sudden acceleration. The guys are bearing down on you at top speed. They've been running flat out in a straight line. It's hard for them to change direction. It's hard for them to get you if you can get on the side of them, running right back 'against the grain.'"

Returning punts or kickoffs, the runner usually has a wedge of blockers in front of him as he moves out. This wedge may take care of a few defenders for the runner. But once he is in a broken field, he is on his own. His is more of a solo effort than other runners'. His work is explosive and breathtaking—and dangerous. If he runs into a defender going at full tilt, their collision speed may be thirty or even forty miles per hour.

Most teams assign their swiftest non-regular runner to return kicks, relying on sheer sprinter's speed. Yet some of the best return specialists have been more shifty than fast. Haymond, who had run the 100 in 9.9, said, "There are plenty who are faster. I try to outmaneuver people."

Haymond reacted rapidly when he caught the ball, making his moves more by instinct than by plan. But he studied his art and tried to anticipate what moves would work best in a given situation. He used blockers intelligently, but was always ready to go on his own.

"I have a move I picked up from Gale Sayers,

Alvin Haymond clutches the ball and looks downfield, leaving a
fallen opponent in his wake.

Alvin said. "He leans all his weight to one side, then goes the other way. But good defensive backs—guys like Willie Wood and Herb Adderley—they'll sit and wait for the guy. They figure he's leaning that way so he'll go the other way. So I lean right, come up straight, then lean right again, then go left again. I call it my double move." He smiled.

"I also have a move where I look like I'm gonna' fall. I push myself up with one hand and go in the other direction. Once, against Green Bay, I caught a field goal try on the one and got hemmed in at the 15 with six guys around me. I weaved and I weaved and I fell down on one hand. I went two or three steps with my hand on the ground, came out of there and went 55 to set up a touchdown."

Then he showed a look of disgust. "Against Detroit one Thanksgiving Day, I was ready to break open a punt the same way," he said. "But the referee called me for having my knee on the ground." Wistfully, he added, "Fast whistles and penalties nullifying long runs kill the return man."

The best kick-returners seldom go all the way to score. But the long return may set up a score. Haymond said, "I went years waiting for my first one. I'd go 55, 60, 65, 70 yards, but still be stopped short. One guy gets you. After you're free, one guy shouldn't be a problem, but there's always one who is. Often, it's the last man. On punts, it's usually the kicker. On kickoffs, it's usually the safetyman.

"It happens several times a season that you get by ten and the 11th gets you. It's very frustrating. One time against San Francisco, Tommy Davis, the

punter, caught me by the shoelace. I had two
blockers in front of me. Two blockers—and he got
me by the shoelace!"

Alvin shook his head sadly, then grinned. "Now I
put tape on top of my shoes and laces. The only
thing they can get me by now is the socks," he said.

Haymond once had his running shoes dyed deep
green when he was playing for Philadelphia in a
game against the New York Giants in 1966. He
promptly ran back a kickoff 98 yards for a touchdown. A big hole opened up the middle and he burst
through. Crossing the goal line, he held the football
high over his head in one hand, and held up a finger
on the other: it was his first touchdown and he was
Number One.

After the game he sat in front of his locker looking
at the shoes. "I just wanted to try something different," he said. "It kinda' psychs you a little bit—
makes you run a little quicker. It also psychs the
other guys. They say, 'What we got here, green
shoes? Man, they must be fast!' "

He smiled and said, "I've been waiting years for
this. Lo-o-o-ong years." Then he stood up. He
seemed shaky. Later in the game he had been flat-
tened a split-second after catching a punt and now
he was feeling it. "I'm starting to feel bad now," he
said. "I'm gonna' wash my mouthpiece off." Swaying
slightly, he walked off, holding his false teeth in one
hand.

Haymond had had his front teeth knocked loose
by Bob Jeter. Junior Coffey of Atlanta had jarred his
shoulder loose in 1966. For a long time after that,

every time he was hit in the shoulder, it would pop painfully out of the socket and have to be rotated back in. Finally, he had an operation on the shoulder during the pre-season exhibition period in 1967. He missed part of the season but came back as strong as ever.

Usually he jumped right up after being hit. He said, "I do it to psych myself and psych the tackler. I don't want to give in to getting hurt. And a lot of times the tacklers will say something to me, like, 'That ought to slow you up for a while.' Well, I may have been hit a heck of a shot, but I'm not going to let him know it. If I say, 'Is that the hardest you can hit?' and jump right up, it takes the edge off his enthusiasm. Of course, sometimes it may make him mad. You got to pick your spots."

Sometimes they knocked him unconscious. Usually he was merely knocked groggy. Two players would come out onto the field, grab him under the arms and help him off. The trainer would put an ice pack on his neck, wave smelling salts under his nose and ask him questions like, "Are you all right?" or "Who are you?" or "Where are you?" Sooner or later, Alvin could answer. And usually by the next kick, he was ready. "You can condition yourself to come to in a hurry," said Haymond. "There is no reason not to be ready by the time of the next punt."

Haymond's bravery awed most observers. Melvin Durslag, a Los Angeles *Herald-Examiner* columnist, said of Alvin's job: "In the realm of safety, it ranks somewhere between deep-sea diving and motorcy-cle-racing on an outlaw track. . . . There is no ac-

With the Baltimore Colts, Haymond is pounced upon after
returning a punt against Dallas.

counting for taste. Some guys like a fast car. . . .
And then there are those who climb the Matterhorn.
But Alvin, he is seized by a curious excitement each
time the ball is in the air and a company of tacklers
is surrounding him."

Alvin Henry Haymond was born August 31st,

1942, in New Orleans. At L.B. Landry High School he was 5-foot-10 and 170 pounds as a senior and the smallest back on the team. But he was also the best on a team that went undefeated and won the state championship.

Haymond followed a teammate to Southern University, a black school in New Orleans. Despite his speed, he was considered too slow for the track team. But he was fast enough to run with the football team.

Baltimore picked him on the 18th round of the pro draft. Almost all the good players and a lot of the bad players had already been chosen. No scout knew much about him: he wasn't well known. He was a 6-foot 195-pounder with no obvious special skills. The Colts were "drawing blind" when they chose him.

Few players chosen that late make it in pro ball. Few are even given a chance to make it. But Haymond turned out to be one of those rare "sleepers" who come into pro ball and upset the experts.

The one asset Haymond had was courage. He said he learned to be tough growing up in his poor neighborhood. "Where I was living, the parks were quite a distance from my house, so we used to play in the street, or in between the highway—a strip about 20 feet wide. In my environment, we didn't know how to play anything easy—we'd knock heads and roll each other in the dirt, and, boy, you had to be tough. We'd fall into the street and get all messed up. I have scars on my face right now from falling in the street. There were a lot of boys who came up the same way."

As a rookie in the NFL Haymond got to play little. He was used as a defensive reserve and ran back only one punt and one kickoff. His second season he was turned into a return specialist, and eventually he became a regular defensive back.

Most specialists do not handle both punts and kickoffs, but Alvin did. Usually he carried punts to the sidelines and kickoffs down the middle, but he varied his approach so he couldn't be typed. Modern defensive formations placed the punter far back and freed the linemen to rush downfield. This reduced the number of exciting punt returns to a minimum. Haymond said sometimes he preferred these punts because he caught the ball in a crowd of teammates and defenders and was not so open a target.

In 1965, his second year in pro ball, Haymond led the league in punt returns with 41, a league record, and yards gained on punt returns, 403. He also gained 614 yards on 20 kickoff returns, averaging more than 30 yards an attempt. Altogether he gained more than 1,000 yards. In 1966 he again led in punt returns, 40, and yardage, 347, but got to handle only 10 kickoffs, which he returned 223 yards.

After his shoulder operation in 1967 he played only enough to total 481 yards on runbacks. But in 1968 he got 201 yards on 15 punts and 677 yards on 28 kickoffs.

Prior to the 1968 season he was traded to Philadelphia for Tim Brown, one of the best running backs of modern times, who was nearing retirement. In his first season with the Eagles Haymond missed three games with injuries, but returned 15 punts for

201 yards and 28 kickoffs for 677 yards. Traded to Los Angeles for three players before the 1969 season, Alvin carried on 33 punt-returns for 435 yards and his third NFL title in this department. He also returned 16 kickoffs for 375 yards. In 1970 he returned 53 punts for 376 yards, second highest in the league. He topped the league in kickoff returns with 35 for 1,022 yards, including a 98-yard scoring runback.

Not all coaches recognize the value of the specialist kick returner. Rather than take up room on the roster with a man who would run back kicks four or five or six times a game, they give this job to a defensive back. Thus they are able to keep an extra substitute at another position. Yet more games are broken open and settled by the runback man's skill than by just about any other man on a squad. Alvin Haymond would have been uniquely valuable if he did nothing else but return kicks, but he has preserved a place for himself by proving an effective defensive back as well.

With Baltimore he was once named outstanding defensive player of the week after leading his team to a triumph over San Francisco. Haymond ran back four kicks for 97 yards. Midway in the first half he made a diving interception of a John Brodie pass to stymie the 49ers on the Colt one-yard-line. Later he cut in front of receiver Dave Parks to pick off another Brodie toss and thus set up the decisive Colt touchdown. And he made five unassisted tackles, some of them bone-rattling wallops, and was in on a dozen more stops.

After the game San Francisco coach Christiansen said, "Haymond turned the game around all by himself. Few players in this league can hurt you so many ways." Baltimore coach Don Shula said, "He's one of the toughest players in the circuit."

In Los Angeles Haymond was an irregular, yet he earned special praise from his coach, George Allen: "Alvin is first on the field, last off and is continually doing things to help others. That's why he's captain of our special teams. He does dirty jobs with enthusiasm. He's a good all-around football player and a great kick returner."

Sighing, Haymond said, "I guess most players would want to be a regular running back, a star who gets a lot of recognition, but I just like to play and I figure being a specialist makes me special.

"I guess you could say I've got a lot of guts, doing the thing I do. There are some who say I'm crazy. I remember once one Minnesota guy hit me on a punt return and he says to me, 'If you think you're crazy now, wait till we finish with you today.' It's like they're going to damage me bad. But they can't scare me. I'm still here. And I don't want people to go around thinking I'm nuts. I'm just good at a job someone has to do. Most who try don't last long at it. I've lasted. I've been hurt, but I'm still alive. So I do my thing and the big-name fullbacks and halfbacks do theirs and I've outlasted a lot of them."

Playing with the Philadelphia Eagles, Haymond tackles Don Perkins (43) of the Dallas Cowboys.

RON JOHNSON

· 8 ·

RON JOHNSON WAS overshadowed by others most of his life. He grew up in Detroit, the youngest of five children, and went through high school desperately trying to emulate the feats of two athletically-inclined older brothers. Arthur was seven years older than Ron, and Alex was five years older. As a college football star at Michigan, Ron set school and national records, but was outshone by O.J. Simpson of Southern California and Leroy Keyes of Purdue. He did not even make All-America teams.

As a rookie pro for the Cleveland Browns, Johnson broke in brilliantly as a replacement for the injured veteran star, Leroy Kelly. But when Kelly returned, Ron slipped back into the shadows. He was eventually traded to the New York Giants.

In 1970 brother Alex batted .329 for the California Angels and won the American League baseball batting championship by a fraction of a percentage point over Carl Yastrzemski of the Boston Red Sox. Meanwhile, Ron became the first runner in the long history of the New York Giants to gain more than 1,000 yards in a single season. Still, he finished only second in the National Conference rushing race, gaining only about 100 yards less than Larry Brown of the Washington Redskins.

Although he finished second in the 1970 rushing race, Ron Johnson still emerged as a superstar. A versatile runner and pass-catcher, he sparked the Giants' return to contention as one of pro football's top teams. Ron became an important man in New York and looked forward to a brilliant future. "I've felt all along I could play with the best," he said. "Some fellows just aren't in the right place at the right time. Some fellows never get the attention and glory others get. The important thing is getting your chances and doing the job. I'm sure everything will work out fine for me in the future."

Ronald Adolphus Johnson was born October 17th, 1947. His father had a trucking business in Detroit. "We didn't have it bad," Ron recalled. "When I was a kid I had all I wanted. But my father had only a fourth-grade education and he wanted more for his children. He was a great inspiration to us. I had two older brothers who were an inspiration to me. Arthur and Alex were both my idols. We always played sports. You name it and we played it—baseball, basketball, football, even ice hockey. I always wanted to be as good as they were."

Arthur deserted sports to join the family business, but Alex went on. Ron recalled that when he was a boy, Alex made him pitch to him until he was so

weary he wept. "We had a game called 'strikeout.'
We would mark a strike zone on a wall and try to
strike each other out with a tennis ball. Alex would
put me maybe 25 feet from him and he would have
me pitch. I'd throw for maybe two hours. My arm
would be hurting and I would start crying. Alex
would tell me, 'Only a couple more pitches.' " The
practice paid off for Alex, but it turned Ron to football.

Ron said, "When I was a kid and they said, 'What
are you going to be—banker, lawyer, Indian chief?' I
never said I was going to be a pro football player. I
never dreamed I'd be that good. . . . Because of
Alex, we were a baseball oriented family. Because of
Alex, baseball scouts hung around me. They tried to
shove me into it. It got to be too much for me. It got
on my nerves. So I began to concentrate on football.
. . . But I wasn't one of these fellows who are super-
stars right from the start. I had to work at it. I had to
improve."

He became good enough at Northwestern High
School in Detroit to get a football scholarship to the
University of Michigan. However, in his first varsity
season as a sophomore, he got to play only 29 minutes, carrying the ball only 12 times for 44 yards. His
second season, 1967, he made the first team and exploded into prominence by running for 270 yards
against Navy, shaking loose on individual runs of 51,
62 and 72 yards. He wound up the season with 1,005
yards, setting a new single-season school record. He
was voted Michigan's Most Valuable Player and
made the Big Ten All-Star Team.

In his senior year Johnson became the first black
captain in Wolverine football history. End Jim Man-
dich said, "He's a fantastic inspiration to our team.
I've never seen a guy more dedicated to our cause.
In a quiet way, he gets the message across to all of
us." Quarterback Denny Brown said, "Though he
seems mostly quiet, when he says something, we all
listen. And he can lift up our ball club without
saying anything, just by the way he does things. He's
a born leader."

"I just try to do everything right," Ron shrugged.
"It comes natural to me to work hard. When I'm on
the field, I give it everything I have. And I'm all for
the team. I'll sacrifice for the team. Every good
player will. Nothing you do amounts to much if it
doesn't help your team. What matters is winning."

Bennie Oosterban, Michigan's former coach, was
particularly impressed with a play Johnson made
against Indiana: "He's always the first guy down
under punts. This time he hit the receiver, but the
guy shook loose. Ron was on his hands and knees,
but he literally scratched his way to get back at the
guy and he got him. I don't ever recall another in-
stance of extra effort quite like that. Johnson makes a
lot of big plays that stand out, but he also makes a lot
of great little plays that maybe don't get noticed but
count for a lot."

In his last year of college ball Ron made many big
plays and had many big games. He gained 110 yards
against Navy. He gained 152 yards against Michigan
State. He gained 174 against Indiana. He gained 205
against Duke. He set an NCAA one-game record by

Michigan's Ron Johnson dives over a jam-up against the
University of Minnesota.

gaining 347 yards, including five touchdowns, against Wisconsin. In the season's finale, against awesome Ohio State, he charged through the Buckeye defenders for 91 yards, winding up with a new single-season record of 1,221 yards. His career total of 2,440 yards also set a school record. He repeated as Michigan MVP and was also named Big Ten MVP.

He had been clocked in 9.8 seconds in the 100-yard dash, which is fast for all but the fastest sprinters. However, some pro scouts said he wasn't fast enough in a football uniform. Simpson and Keyes were the first two players chosen in the pros' draft of graduating college seniors. Nineteen players were chosen before Cleveland's turn came up, and the Browns picked Ron.

Simpson and Keyes signed such fabulous bonus contracts that Ron was disappointed when Cleveland offered him only $50,000 a season for two seasons. He hired a powerful attorney to negotiate with the Browns for him. He held out for a bigger contract all summer and well into the exhibition season and missed the annual College All-Star Game. Finally, he fired his attorney and signed.

He explained, "I felt I deserved more money, but I also felt I had to sign soon if I was going to make it my first year in the pros. I had looked forward a long time to playing in the All-Star Game and I regretted missing that a lot. I felt that if I missed anything more important, I might regret it all my life."

When Ron finally did arrive in Cleveland, he made it clear what he was there for. Coach Blanton

Collier said, "He just came in and said, 'Let's play football.' He went to work and proved himself. He proved to be a total football player who can run, catch and block. He started late, but worked hard to catch up. He's a hard worker."

By the opening game of the 1969 season Johnson was in the injured Leroy Kelly's regular halfback slot. He carried 17 times for 118 yards, including one run for 48 yards. He also caught two passes, one on an acrobatic, tumbling reception. He gained more than 100 yards in the second game, too. Suddenly he was a sensation. However, Kelly returned to action for the third game and was restored to his regular role. Johnson was shifted to fullback. Although 6-foot-1 and 205 pounds, he was small by pro standards for a fullback and had never played that position before. He began to fade.

By the season's end he had gained only 471 yards and no longer was considered a regular. During the off-season he was traded with tackle Jim Kanicki and linebacker Wayne Meylan to the Giants for flashy veteran end Homer Jones. With Kelly healthy, the Browns considered Johnson expendable. "I really was shocked by the trade," Ron admitted. "It always bothers a player when someone doesn't want him, and to be let go so soon. . . .

"But I'd had my problems. Once Kelly came back, I was pushed into the background. With Kelly in the backfield, you don't carry much. . . . Mostly they

Beginning his pro career with the Cleveland Browns, Johnson blocks for Leroy Kelly (44) against the Detroit Lions.

expected blocking from me. I had got off to such a great start, I guess everyone expected too much from me too soon. I guess I expected too much from myself. When I didn't get the chance to do as much, I grew discouraged. After playing exhibition games, by the fifth or sixth pro game I felt like I'd played a full season by college standards and there still was more than half the season to go. I got tired and I had lost all confidence. I kept playing, but I wasn't getting any better. They were disappointed in this. But I was pressing too hard. I was just too inexperienced."

In New York in 1970 the second-year man was determined to prove himself as a pro. And the Giants were hungry for a good halfback. They gave Johnson plenty of work and profited from it enormously. He worked hard and improved steadily. He had a lot of good games and a few great ones. One came against Philadelphia. He gained 142 yards in 18 carries. He had touchdown runs of 34 and 68 yards. He had one even longer, 87 yards, but it was called back on a penalty. He had slipped around right end, eluded a linebacker, broken a tackle, and sprinted all the way before an illegal procedure call cancelled the tremendous run.

"It's all part of the game," he shrugged later. "I got it back, though, when we really needed it," he added. He had broken loose for the 34-yard touchdown run with only 49 seconds remaining. His score broke a 23–23 tie and gave the Giants a 30–23 triumph. Quarterback Fran Tarkenton said the play had been called in an attempt to move the Giants

closer for a late field-goal attempt and he was startled when Ron carried it across the goal line. Johnson, himself, admitted he wasn't thinking of a touchdown: "I had no thought of a long run. We needed
yards and I was trying to get them. I went right into
the line. I just hit quick and hard, and suddenly it
opened up. I got great blocking. I could have walked
in. Some touchdowns come when you least expect
them. An ordinary play, if executed perfectly, can
break a game wide open."

Breaking this early-season game wide open
seemed to restore Ron's confidence in himself, and
he was hard for opposing teams to handle from then
on. In a critical game against Dallas Ron ripped
through their famed "Doomsday Defense" for 136
yards. On one 71-yard drive he personally ran for 63
of the yards. Still, the Giants trailed 20–16. Late in
the contest, when they took over on their own 27,
Ron performed at his peak. Tarkenton passed to
Clifton McNeil for 32 yards, ran Ron for two, then
passed to Ron for 22 and a first down at the Dallas
17. Tarkenton scrambled for four yards, but then
missed on a pass and came to a critical third-down
call. He had his two top receivers, McNeil and Johnson, run a cross-pattern. Johnson shook loose Dallas'
great defensive back, Mel Renfro, and took a 13-
yard toss for the triumphant touchdown.

With Tarkenton scrambling skillfully and Johnson
running and receiving brilliantly, the Giants went
into their final regular-season game, against Los Angeles, with a chance for a divisional pennant. And
Johnson went into the climactic contest with a

Traded to the New York Giants, Johnson breaks into the clear
to receive this pass in a game against the St. Louis Cardinals.

chance to gain more than 1,000 yards for the season. Unfortunately, the powerful Rams pushed the Giants all over the field. But Johnson gained 43 of the Giants' 50 yards gained rushing. He passed the 1,000-yard mark and totaled more yards in a single season than Frank Gifford or any other runner in the Giants' history.

Johnson ranked second in rushing in the conference, and eighth in pass receiving with 48 catches for 487 yards. He was the only player in either conference to rank in the top ten in both rushing and receiving. He topped all performers in total yardage from scrimmage with more than 1,500 yards. Tarkenton concluded, "He is the best halfback in football. He does everything. He blocks. He catches the ball. He runs inside and outside. And he makes the big plays. All the great ones make the big plays. He is a great one and he is going to get greater."

Not long ago Johnson reflected on his experience in the NFL. "I expected the players in this league to be bigger, stronger and faster than any I had faced before," he said, "and I wasn't surprised. I was surprised at how aggressive all the defensive players were. They never seem to give up on a play and they hit hard. In college I could break most tackles easily. In pro ball I've found there are none that are broken easily. Instead of one or two outstanding players on every team, every player on every team is skilled and tough. It takes a lot of extra effort to break tackles and gain extra yards. I've had to learn to concentrate at all times and go all out on every step of every play.

"Being able to catch the ball has helped me a lot. I have enough speed and moves to get open and good hands to hold on to passes and when I get the ball, I can go with it. But I am primarily a runner. It helps me that the defense is never sure whether I'm going to run the ball or go out for a pass. They can't play me as tight as if I was only a runner.

"I'm still making a lot of mistakes. I'm my own worst critic. I seldom leave a game thinking I couldn't have done a whole lot better. But I am correcting my mistakes as fast as I can and cutting down on them as much as I can. Two years of pro ball, playing regular my second year, knowing my team counted on me, has helped bring out the best in me. I think now that, barring injuries, which always are a threat, I have a chance to have a good and long career in pro football."

A bright, personable fellow, Ron was an excellent student and graduated from college with a degree in marketing and finance. Later he did some off-season work in banking. He celebrated his success in 1970 by marrying his college sweetheart, the former Karen Lyons, less than a week after the Giants lost their last game to the Rams.

Ron said he was not too deeply disappointed to miss the post-season championship contests. He was only in his second season as a pro, and he hoped eventually to help his team win a Super Bowl during the 70s. "We came from way out to become contenders in one season and felt we accomplished a lot. I came from nowhere into prominence this one season, myself, and feel I accomplished a lot. It was a

Johnson escapes the reaching hand at left and moves with classic grace downfield.

letdown, no question of that, to lose the last game and have it all over all of a sudden, but I think we set ourselves up for some fine years in the future."

An excellent speaker, Ron became a prominent representative of the Giants at banquets and meetings around New York. He had a markedly different personality from that of his brother Alex, who seldom spoke to his teammates, the writers, or the fans.

Alex was often curt to outsiders and was branded as a tough, temperamental, mean fellow who hurt the morale of his team. Despite consistent hitting, he was traded three times in five seasons.

"I don't agree with Alex's attitude," Ron admit-ted. "I've seen the way he behaves in baseball. He is introverted. He does not like attention. He wants to go his own way. If he thinks something, he says it. I respect the fact that he is not a hypocrite and does what he wants to do, but I do think sometimes he comes on too strong. I must say he's never shown anything to me or our family but kindness. I know he has shown another side of himself to others. I think it's unfortunate. I think it hinders his career. I think I've learned from his mistakes. I go out of my way to get along with people. We are brothers, but we are different people and different personalities. I do my thing and he does his."

Ron Johnson was traded once. He didn't want to be traded again. "In my case, I'm sure I wasn't traded because of my attitude. I was told I was traded because the club felt it was a deal it had to make, because it needed help at other positions more than it needed help at mine. Once I accepted it, I could see it was the best possible thing for me. There is no city in which an athlete has more oppor-tunities for his future than New York and none in which an outstanding fellow gets more attention. There are a lot of good running backs in football. I'm one of them. I have a chance to be outstanding. I'm not the only one who has had to struggle to gain the limelight."

CALVIN HILL & DUANE THOMAS

·9·

IN 1969 CALVIN HILL, the halfback of the Dallas Cowboys, had been NFL Rookie of the Year. Then early in the 1970 season Hill was sidelined with injuries. Much to the surprise of the Cowboys, Duane Thomas, a 1970 rookie, stepped into Hill's halfback position to stay. He carried the ball for 803 yards during the remainder of the campaign and Dallas captured a divisional pennant. Thomas' average of better than five yards a carry was the best in pro football.

When Dallas entered the playoffs, Calvin Hill had recovered, but his job now belonged to Duane Thomas. Hill stood sadly on the sidelines while Thomas tore up the playing field. First Dallas nosed out Detroit 5–0 in a defenseive struggle. The Cowboys were able to pass for only 22 yards, but they controlled the ball because of Thomas, who carried the ball 30 times for 135 yards. His short, savage run on a critical third-down play set up the only score in the first three quarters, a Dallas field-goal.

Then in the NFC championship game Dallas met San Francisco. Thomas was the star once again, carrying 27 times for 143 yards. Time after time, Thomas took quarterback Craig Morton's pitchouts and loped through or around the San Francisco right side. The 49ers led 3–0 in the second quarter when Thomas caught fire: he carried eight times for 56 yards and caught a pass for 14 yards to set up a Dallas field goal that tied the game. Then early in the third period Duane took a handoff at the 49ers' 13-yard-line on a play over right tackle. Seeing the right side blocked off, Thomas cut to his left, broke a tackle, turned toward the goal-line, stepped around a defensive back and drove into the end zone to put Dallas ahead 10–3. The Cowboys went on to win 17–10.

In his first year Thomas had become "the best running back in pro football," according to Bob Oates of the Los Angeles *Times*. Duane Thomas had no false modesty. He said himself that he was "the greatest runner around." He was suddenly a celebrity and Dallas was headed for the Super Bowl. Thomas seemed certain to win 1970s Rookie of the Year laurels.

In the meantime Calvin Hill, who had been a celebrity the year before, was sitting on the bench. He must have wondered what had happened to *his* fans and how long Thomas' glory would last. Calvin Hill was born in Baltimore, an only child of poor, hard-working parents. "I guess you could call the neighborhood where I spent my childhood a ghetto," he said. "It was a black neighborhood and all the houses

Against the San Francisco 49ers, the Cowboys' Duane Thomas picks his way through crowded territory.

were old, but there were plenty of good, hard-working people living there."

From the beginning Calvin loved sports. His father, Henry, recalled, "From the time he was old enough to walk, he always wanted me to play catch with him. He got a baseball glove when he was five and baseball shoes when he was six. I used to play a

lot of sandlot baseball when I was a young man and
at one time I thought my son might become a professional baseball player. And he was good enough in
school to have become one. But he grew very big
and found football was his best game."

Calvin was more than just an athlete. He was a
Cub Scout and a Boy Scout, attended church regularly with his parents and got straight A's in school.
His mother said, "He was never any problem about
studying. He'd come in the door, put his books on a
table and sit down and start. Then he'd go out and
play. He was very fast with school things." Calvin's
family doctor, Dr. William Wade, and a neighborhood recreation center leader, Oceola Smith, recognized Cal's special abilities. They recommended to
his parents that he apply to a fine college preparatory school, the Riverdale Country School in New
York City.

Calvin applied and was accepted, receiving a
Schenley Foundation scholarship. At Riverdale he
was outstanding in baseball, basketball and track, as
well as in football. Guided by an outstanding coach,
Frank Bertino, Cal became a fine quarterback,
throwing 15 touchdown passes in his senior season.
He also achieved a high grade average.

His combination of scholarship and athletic ability
brought many college scholarship offers. Many big-
time football colleges were interested in him, but he
chose to go to Yale, one of the finest educational in-
stitutions in the country. Yale's football teams play
in the Ivy League and rarely send players on to professional careers. But Hill was thinking about more

than pro football. "I knew I couldn't play football forever," he said, "and I wanted to go to the best school which would give me the best education for the future."

At Yale he continued to be a good student, majoring in history. He also joined black student groups, was a deacon in the student chapel and was active in campus religious affairs. He wanted to make the church his life's work eventually, although he was not sure he wanted to study for the ministry.

"Possibly I would prefer to work for the church in some other capacity," he said. "I know I would like to help modernize church work. The church needs to be more socially active, more involved in everyday life. It can't be just a Sunday thing. And I believe the black church can contribute more to the black community than it has." After he graduated from Yale and signed up with the Cowboys, he enrolled at a summer school of theology at Southern Methodist University in Dallas.

At Yale Hill had been converted from quarterback to running back. Yale's outstanding quarterback, Brian Dowling, was white and Hill was black. Since there have been few black quarterbacks in college football and none who ever played regularly in pro football, Hill wondered at first if he had been shifted because of his color. But eventually he concluded, "I was a much better halfback than Brian could have been and we were a much better team with both me and Brian in the same backfield, and we won regularly, so I'm satisfied the move was justified." With Dowling passing and Hill running, Yale lost only one game in Hill's junior and senior seasons.

At 6-foot-4 and 220 pounds, Hill obviously had pro potential. Still, many scouts were unsure of him because the Ivy League competition was not as tough as in some major conferences. Some felt he might be a better tight end than a halfback. Dallas drafted Hill on the first round after 22 teams had passed him over. Dallas gave a special intelligence and psychology test to all of its prospects. Hill had scored in the top two per cent of the 4,000 men who had ever taken it. The Cowboys were convinced they had a fine prospect, but they, too, were planning to make him a tight end.

Then Hill got his chance in the opening game of the 1969 season, against San Francisco. The regular Cowboy running backs, Dan Reeves and Walt Garrison, were injured. Calvin played in the backfield and ran around, through and over the 49ers for 106 yards to set up a 20–17 triumph. Said coach Tom Landry, "We've never had a rookie step in and play like that before. We were all excited."

In the season's second game, against New Orleans, Dallas was trailing with five minutes to go. From the Saints' five Hill ran into the line, was stopped, spun free, was hit hard at the three, tore loose, and leaped through the air and over the goal line for the winning points in a 21–17 victory. He had run 23 yards for an earlier score and had gained 138 yards for the game setting a new team record. "Man, it was rough out there," he admitted later. "It was as tough as the Yale-Harvard game," he added with a smile.

In the third game of the season he played only in

Calvin Hill sits dejectedly on the sidelines, watching Dallas lose to Cleveland 38–14.

the first half. He had set up an easy victory, running 91 yards in 10 carries, catching three passes for 44 yards and throwing one for 44 yards, before being benched by an ankle injury. One of his runs carried him 53 yards. He came back in the fourth game to run for 150 yards and total 285 yards, running and receiving, as Dallas routed the Washington Redskins.

After one game Calvin's father, Henry, met Dan

Reeves, whose halfback job Calvin had taken. Reeves said, "Mr. Hill, I just want to tell you what a fine boy you have. He plays the same position I do, and you're not supposed to like someone who can keep you on the bench, but I guarantee you, we're glad to have him."

Henry Hill was happy with this, but not surprised. He recalled a visit to Dallas during the off-season in which Coach Landry said, "Ivy League players never have done much in pro football, but maybe Calvin can prove he's different."

"Coach," said the elder Hill, "there's not going to be any 'maybe' about Calvin."

Later, Landry told writers, "Calvin Hill may be the finest running back I've seen in 20 years. He makes the big play game after game."

Calvin Hill, himself, said, "Whatever I am, my blockers have made me. Any back could gain a lot of yards behind the Dallas line. If O.J. Simpson had the line I had, he'd gain 3,000 yards."

Calvin was willing to settle for 1,000 yards and the league rushing championship in his rookie year. But in a game with Washington, he broke a bone in his foot. Suddenly, and painfully, his fortunes changed. "It was strange," he recalled. "I remember running the ball and going back into the huddle and then taking my stance in the backfield and I didn't feel a thing. Then we went into a formation switch and suddenly I felt the pain. My whole foot hurt, especially my big toe. It wasn't like I was hit or anything, and I still can't figure out how it happened."

Blisters developed and infection set in as he tried

Hill jumps over one Atlanta Falcon tackler into the arms of another.

to run unnaturally to compensate for the pain. He finished the year with 946 yards and in second place to Gale Sayers' 1,032 yards in the NFL's final rushing statistics. After the season he had an operation to repair the damage in his foot. But then early in 1970 he injured his leg and his shoulder. He gained 117 yards against Philadelphia, but then was benched by his injuries.

Hill's misfortune gave Duane Thomas his chance. Hill regained his health, but not his regular job. As Dallas worked its way to the post-season playoffs, Thomas ran for 803 yards, Hill for 577 yards, and regular fullback Walt Garrison for 507 yards. No team in football had better running backs, but Hill had become a substitute. There were rumors that he would be converted to end after all. Coach Landry had changed his tune. Now he was saying, "Duane Thomas is one of the greatest rookie runners I've ever seen."

Duane Thomas grew up in the Dallas area. When he was in high school, both his parents died. For a while the family split up. Duane lived in Los Angeles with an aunt for some time and then moved some more. "Man, like I traveled and saw things," he said. He returned to Dallas to finish high school, then received a football scholarship to West Texas State. There, he blocked for and played in the shadow of running back "Mercury" Morris. Still, he gained 2,378 yards rushing, and averaged more than six yards a run in three seasons of play.

Most pro scouts underrated Thomas' prospects, although Hampton Pool, the chief scout for Los Angeles, called him the best all-around pro prospect he had ever seen, even better than Jim Brown. But the Rams' coach, George Allen, wanted a linebacker, so he passed up Thomas. Dallas picked Duane on the first round. Like Hill the year before, Thomas was the 23rd player chosen. Dallas had a top-notch halfback in Hill. But the Cowboys' philosophy was to pick the most talented player regardless of position.

When Hill was hurt, the 6-foot-2, 220-pound Thomas got his chance and made the most of it. He ran for 79 yards against the mighty Minnesota defense. He then ran 134 yards, including a 47-yard scoring burst on a draw play, against the strong Kansas City Chiefs. Against Washington he was kneed in the head on the opening kickoff and had to be helped off the field. But he returned to gain 104 yards, including a spectacular 35-yard scoring run down the sideline.

Yet there were moments when Dallas coaches thought they had sent a madman forth. Thomas occasionally dropped the ball and dribbled or kicked it out of bounds, especially on kickoffs. Against New York he had a 101-yard touchdown run locked up and was out in the clear when he decided to shift the ball from one hand to the other. Somehow he threw it out of bounds. But he kept gaining game after game, picking up 123 yards in a rematch with Washington and 115 against Houston when Dallas clinched its divisional title.

Thomas was hard-pressed to explain his running style. It seemed to vary from run to run. "I don't think about things, I just do them," he said. Dallas

Duane Thomas peers through his face guard after being felled
by a Detroit Lion tackler.

coaches said, "Whatever it takes, he seems to have.
He's our best blocking back and he follows blockers
very well. He has the strength to run right through
tacklers and the quickness and speed to dart past
them or run away from them."

A most natural and unorthodox young man, he
swiftly became a big star in Dallas. He was a frustrated rock-and-roll singer and was considered something of a loner. Yet he wasn't bothered by the attention. "When you're the best, you have to expect
attention," he said. When a white schoolgirl asked
the black star to write something in her autograph

book, he wrote, "Dear Linda . . . Don't hate black, don't hate white . . . When you get bit, just hate to bite." Then he told her he had borrowed that from Sly and the Family Stone, a rock group, and went on his way.

After helping the Cowboys win their playoff games against Detroit and San Francisco, Thomas was matched against another surprising rookie star in the Super Bowl—Norm Bulaich of Baltimore.

Like many other young players, Bulaich got his chance when a regular was injured. Baltimore's ten-year veteran running back Tom Matte had been injured early in the 1970 season. Bulaich, who had been handicapped by injuries throughout his college career at Texas Christian, had not been well-known when he entered pro ball. After rushing for 426 yards in Matte's spot during the regular season, Bulaich had exploded into prominence by running for 116 yards in Baltimore's first playoff game. But in the Super Bowl, neither star did well. Dallas limited Bulaich to 28 yards on 18 carries, while Baltimore limited Thomas to 37 yards in 18 carries.

After the season, in an appearance on Merv Griffin's late-night television show, it was suggested to Thomas that he should be wary of someone coming along to take his job the way he had taken Hill's.

"No way," Thomas replied. "No one can replace me."

Before replying, Thomas might have considered Hill's case once more. Pro football runners are in a risky business and none of them can guarantee his future.

LARRY BROWN

· 10 ·

LARRY BROWN WAS born deaf in his right ear. He wanted to be a baseball player, but he concentrated on football because it was a way to get a college scholarship.

Brown played two years of football for a high school team that won only two games in that time. He was not All-State or All-City or even All-League. After graduation he was lucky to get a chance to go to a small junior college, where he was used as a blocker, not a runner.

Larry eventually went on to a senior college and played football, but only as a blocker for a star runner on a mediocre team. He rarely ran and rarely got a chance to catch passes. He was not All-America or All-League, or all anything. He was drafted by the Washington Redskins in the eighth round of the draft, after almost 250 others had been selected.

In the Redskin training camp at Carlisle, Pennsylvania, the great, tough coach, Vince Lombardi, was in his first season as coach of the Redskins. Larry

Brown was only one of 21 running backs who would try out for a place on the team, and few thought he would make it.

At one point in the practice, during a passing drill, Brown dropped a couple of tosses. Vince Lombardi turned to assistant coach Bill Austin and said, "He can't play for me; he can't catch the ball."

Lombardi was especially depressed with how slowly Brown reacted to the snap of the ball and how often he seemed to not know the plays. And to round out the dismal impression, Larry weighed less than 200 pounds.

Brown recalled, "I was on the wrong side of the huddle and couldn't always hear the play called. I couldn't hear the quarterback call signals and had to wait until I saw the center snap the ball before I moved. I wasn't always sure which way to go, and if the ball was thrown to me, I sometimes was surprised."

Finally, Lombardi demanded one day, "Do you know the plays?"

"Yes, sir," Brown said.

"Well, what's the matter? Do you have trouble hearing?"

"Yes, sir," Brown admitted.

Lombardi was startled. He called Brown into conference and discovered that Brown was deaf in his right ear. He had gotten by with the defect previously, but in the demanding environment of a pro camp, it was hurting his performance.

Lombardi changed things immediately. He placed Brown on the quarterback's right side so his words

went into Larry's left ear. He also had a tiny, transistorized hearing aid inserted into Larry's helmet, enabling him to hear on the right side. A few years earlier the NFL had banned wiring players for sound, but Lombardi prevailed upon NFL Commissioner Pete Rozelle to allow a hearing aid in Brown's hardship case.

"I remember when he first gave me the hearing aid," Brown said. "He took me to a room and stood me at the opposite end from him and asked me if I could hear him. I said, 'Coach, I could always hear *you.*' Frankly, Lombardi spoke in a roar and it was hard not hearing him. He laughed about that. But with the aid, I could hear others as well as Lombardi."

Larry Brown struggles to keep
his balance after eluding a
Baltimore tackler.

Once he got his helmet hearing aid, he reacted to
the signal-caller's cadence like a coiled spring, and
he had his plays down pat. Suddenly everything
started to click for Brown. He won a permanent position in the Redskin backfield, and by the season's
end, he was fourth in NFL rushing with 888 yards,
averaging more than four yards per carry. Rookie of
the Year Calvin Hill of Dallas was the only rookie
runner to rush for more yards, 942.

Brown was born September 19th, 1947, in Clair-
ton, Pennsylvania, one of three sons in the family.
His father, a baggage handler for the Pennsylvania
Railroad, moved them to Pittsburgh when Larry was
young. He grew up in a slum called the "Hill Dis-

trict," and he did not have a great deal.

However, he did have great athletic ability. He was best at baseball when he was young, but in Schenley High School he turned to football as the best bet for his future. Willard Fisher was his coach there, and although the team was terrible, Fisher helped Larry a great deal.

Lacking good grades or outstanding football credentials, Larry had little chance to be recruited by a top college. Fisher found a junior college that would take a chance on Brown. Larry was pleased. He admitted he was anxious to get away from Pittsburgh and see some of the country. Brown received and accepted a scholarship to Dodge City (Kansas) Junior College, where coach Leroy Montgomery used him as a blocking back. Brown did well.

However, after two years at junior college Brown was still not attracting the attention of the big colleges. Brown had a chance to go to Southern Illinois, but when Montgomery landed a job as freshman coach at Kansas State University, he offered Brown a berth and Larry followed him there.

Kansas State was one of the weakest teams in the Big Eight conference then, but it did have a league-leading rusher in Cornelius Davis. Vince Gibson, Kansas' tough varsity coach, who seemed to style himself after Lombardi, used Brown to block for Davis. Without complaint, Larry did his job.

Brown rushed for only 282 yards as a junior and only 402 as a senior, so he seemingly had little to offer pro scouts. However, they were always on the lookout for "sleepers." A few scouts indicated they

liked Larry's blocking, his love of contact, his tough-
ness and his running potential. After the bigger
names were gone, Washington took a chance and
drafted him.

The competition was stiff at the Redskin training
camp, and Brown was, at first, unimpressive. Lombardi said, "I'm not sure what it was that made me
keep looking at the boy, maybe the desire he
showed, but he was having troubles and I couldn't
figure out why."

Lombardi was known for his rugged practices. He
was especially tough when he took over Washington.
The team had been a loser for years. In his first pre-
season drill one player suffered a broken arm, another got his nose broken, and two others received
knee injuries. It was survival of the fittest.

Larry Brown, only 5-foot-11 and 195 pounds,
worked hard and butted heads with players much
bigger than he without complaint and without giving
ground. He set his clock 15 minutes ahead so he
would never be even 15 seconds late for a meeting.
He was the first man on the field for practice and the
last to leave.

Lombardi had a drill in which he set bags full of
foam rubber in two rows four yards apart, forming a
narrow "field." Runners followed a minimum of
blockers through this thin channel, running against a
maximum of tacklers, who kept coming at the ball-
carriers one after another. Larry Brown blasted
down this road time after time in sweltering summer
heat without a single word of protest. In this way he
won himself a chance.

"There was nothing I was not going to do that would help me make the club," he said. "It's all I ever thought about while I was playing college ball, making pro ball, and I was only afraid I wouldn't get the chance. Once I got it, I was determined to make the most of it."

Speaking of Lombardi, Brown said, "He was a very demanding coach. I did some things well and he encouraged me with compliments. But I did other things badly and he yelled at me a lot more than he praised me. He yelled at everyone. He said we were pros and shouldn't make mistakes. He insisted that we make the most of our abilities. He developed a dedication and sense of sacrifice in all of us, and we had the first winning season any Redskin team had in years. I had the desire all along, but I learned a great deal from that man about what it took to play major league football."

The Redskins' backfield coach, Gene Dickson, had high praise for Brown: "He had one big thing going for him: he was hungry. He didn't come in with a big bonus or a big name. He knew he had to work all the time to make an impression and avoid being cut. Sometimes this works to a player's advantage. While the big star is coasting, figuring he has it made, the little guy is hustling. Often, he shoves the big star to the sidelines. The fact is, coaches like to find their own stars. It's more satisfying."

Brown won a place for himself during the exhibition season. Then in his first regular-season game he was nervous and tense and was able to gain only 28 yards running. But in his second game he swept end

Brown is surrounded and thrown to the ground after gaining six yards against the Los Angeles Rams.

for a 57-yard touchdown run and gained 95 yards total. Larry Brown was on his way.

Lombardi died during the off-season and the Redskins fell back a bit under their new coach, Bill Austin, in 1970. But Brown moved ahead. While Calvin Hill, his rookie rival of the prior year, slipped into the shadows, Brown broke all previous Redskin rushing records and became the first back in Redskin history to gain more than 1,000 yards.

Brown led all NFL runners with 1,125 yards in 237 carries, averaging nearly five yards a rush. He caught 37 passes for another 341 yards. Said Austin, "He gives away size and even speed to other backs, but he is big enough and fast enough to do the job and more determined than others."

Brown said, "I'm a competitive person. I hate to see someone else doing something I think I can do. I want to be better. That's why I learned to block early, because some feel I'm too small. I rely on quickness and surprise, trying to hit the rusher before he can defend himself. They're usually bigger and can't move as quick as I can. If it's a 275-pounder, say, I sure can't overpower him, so I just put my head down and go for his legs, his knees. I try to cut him down. If I can't, I stay with him as long as I can to give my quarterback time. On downfield blocking, I try to hit quick. Blocking is technique and desire.

"So is pass-catching. So is running. You practice so you hit the holes the instant they open up, get through them quickly and cut to the open area. You practice so you can make the best possible use of

Larry Brown is all smiles during a Redskin practice.

your blockers. Open-field running is mostly instinct. It's hard to teach. But if a fellow has fair speed and size, he can learn to see what the defense might do and shift speeds and make cuts to confuse tacklers. You never give up. You just go until you're down. Then you get up and go again."

Larry Brown was a handsome young man, 24 years old in 1971. He was so quiet off the field that he was called, with teasing good humor, "Gabby." He liked many things, including jazz, but he was devoted to football. A sociology major in college, he said, "There are other things besides football in life, but as long as football is my life, I will give it everything I have. Barring injuries, which are always a threat, I want to be the best."

George Allen became the Redskins' head coach in 1971. He favored versatile backs, a running game and a balanced attack. He also had a Lombardi-like reputation for winning. In Brown, Allen had one of the finest young performers in the game. Under Allen, Brown had the rare chance to become an established star of the greatest magnitude.

Washington quarterback Sonny Jurgensen said of Brown, "Larry drops passes in practice, but hangs on to them in games. This is the opposite of most players. It's easy for them in practice. They're very flashy in practice. But, come the games, they tense up and fail. The better the test, the better Brown does. The more it counts, the more he does. In tough games, he runs with reckless abandon. He is a most admirable competitor."

There were bigger and faster players than Larry Brown; runners with more natural talent; many who had better hearing; many who were more highly publicized; and many who reached pro football more assured of a place in the spotlight. Still, Brown had made it.

For one year, at least, Larry Brown had been the best runner in pro football. In other years it might be someone else. Floyd Little was just reaching his prime in 1970. O.J. Simpson seemed ready to capture his expected position at the top. From year to year there is no telling who will be on top. Professional football is a difficult and dangerous sport, especially for the running back. It's not easy to make it, and it is perilously easy to fail. But if you make it, you are on top of the world.

INDEX

Page numbers in italics refer to photographs.